Environment at a Glance 2015

OECD INDICATORS

Please cite this publication as:
OECD (2015), *Environment at a Glance 2015: OECD Indicators*, OECD Publishing, Paris.
http://dx.doi.org/10.1787/9789264235199-en

ISBN 978-92-64-23518-2 (print)
ISBN 978-92-64-23519-9 (PDF)
ISBN 978-92-64-23520-5 (HTML)

Photo credits: Cover © iStockphoto.com/JoeGough – Chapter 1 © Stefan Körber/Fotolia.com – Chapter 2 © Inmagine LTD/Don Hammond/Design Pics

Corrigenda to OECD publications may be found on line at: *www.oecd.org/about/publishing/corrigenda.htm*.

Table of contents

Follow OECD Publications on:

 *http://twitter.com/OECD_Pubs*

 *http://www.facebook.com/OECDPublications*

 *http://www.linkedin.com/groups/OECD-Publications-4645871*

 *http://www.youtube.com/oecdilibrary*

http://www.oecd.org/oecddirect/

This book has...

A service that delivers Excel® files from the printed page!

Look for the *StatLinks* at the bottom of the tables or graphs in this book. To download the matching Excel® spreadsheet, just type the link into your Internet browser, starting with the *http://dx.doi.org* prefix, or click on the link from the e-book edition.

Preface

Environment at a glance 2015 *highlights the many OECD countries that have succeeded in reducing their greenhouse gas emissions, and those that have increased their share of renewables in energy supply, improved their waste management, or innovated to more efficiently manage their water resources. The data are there to prove it: whether we are talking about natural resource consumption, waste generation or air emissions, decoupling is possible. These positive developments are attributable both to the rise of the services sector and with it, the displacement of resource- and pollution-intensive production abroad, as well as to policy action and technical progress. The economic crisis also contributed to relieve some pressures on the environment.*

Environment at a Glance *also reveals where progress has slowed or is insufficient. There is substantial scope for strengthening air and climate policies, changing patterns of energy consumption, improving waste and materials management, preserving biodiversity and natural assets, and implementing more integrated policies – all critical components of green growth and sustainable development. Many positive developments still take place at the margin and policies often lack coherence, thus undermining efforts to reduce negative environmental impacts.*

Climate change has been on our agenda for many years. It is now an urgent challenge and a potentially irreversible threat to future economic development and well-being. The carbon intensity of the energy used in human activities has hardly changed since 1990 and fossil fuels continue to dominate energy supply. CO_2 emissions from fuel combustion, calculated by the International Energy Agency, have increased by 36% globally since 2000, in line with global economic growth. With current policies, global energy-related CO_2 emissions are estimated to reach three times the level they need to be at in 2050 to limit the long-term increase in global temperatures to 2°C. More recent estimates indicate a flattening of the CO_2 emission growth rate in 2014, not tied to economic activity. Whether this indicates a new trend remains to be seen in the years to come.

Countries continue to support fossil fuel production and consumption in many ways. Not all fossil fuels are treated equal. Variations in energy tax rates, uneven price signals, low levels of taxation on fuels with high environmental impacts, and exemptions for fuel used in some sectors impede the transition to a low-carbon economy. Coal is usually the least heavily taxed of all fossil fuels but the most carbon-intensive fuel available for electricity generation. This suggests important opportunities for reforming countries' tax systems, aligning policies and achieving environmental goals more cost-effectively.

This is all the more important as the 21st Conference of the Parties to the UN Framework Convention on Climate Change (COP21) will convene in Paris in December 2015. The stakes are high: the aim is to reach a new legally binding international agreement to combat climate change effectively and keep global warming below 2°C. To achieve it, governments and businesses have to urgently confront the challenge of making the transition from a carbon-intensive present to a zero-net carbon future, at a time when many also have to cope with economic challenges and painful trade-offs. It will involve a long-term transformation with structural adjustments and the full engagement of all major economies in the world.

Strong and predictable policies for the decarbonisation of the global economy are needed, with proper price signals and the elimination of environmentally harmful support to producers and consumers, including subsidies that support fossil fuels. Such policies require political will and a long-term view of economic development. They also need to be based on reliable and consistent data that are harmonised at the international level.

Governments, decision makers and civil society need to know how their country is performing, over time and compared to other countries. This is one of the reasons that the OECD has been at the forefront of international efforts to develop environmental indicators since the early 1990s, and green growth indicators since 2011. The OECD also monitors quality of life and well-being as part of its better life initiative. As environmental challenges can seldom be tackled by one country alone, regular monitoring through indicators is used to encourage the sharing of good practices among countries.

There is scope for further improving the information available to assess countries' environmental progress. In many areas, data are weak or missing, and the absence of reliable time series makes it difficult to monitor the effect of policy measures. It is the OECD's task to work with countries to monitor and report on their progress, bearing in mind their specific circumstances. It is also the OECD's task to help countries improve their environmental information systems and produce reliable and coherent indicators.

We will continue to provide governments with harmonised environmental indicators and remain committed to working closely with countries and international partners to improve their quality.

Simon Upton
Director, OECD Environment Directorate

Environment at a Glance 2015
OECD Indicators

Executive summary

Since 2000, progress is visible in emissions of traditional air pollutants, transport fuel efficiency, energy intensity, renewable energy, water use, sewage treatment, and biodiversity protection. This is partly explained by the slowdown in economic activity following the economic crisis, but also by increased uptake by OECD countries of instruments to address environmental pressures, including taxation to influence consumer behaviour and internalise environmental costs. Environmental considerations are also increasingly being mainstreamed in development co-operation and in research and development.

Many of these developments still take place at the margin though, and policies often lack coherence, thus undermining efforts to reduce negative environmental impacts. Countries continue to support fossil fuel production and consumption in many ways, and economic activity remains tied to carbon emissions and wasteful consumption of energy and other natural resources. Major challenges ahead include climate change and the impact of environmental degradation on health and on future growth and development. Robust policies and reliable information are needed to address these challenges, especially as growth resumes.

Key findings

Air pollution continues to be a concern for the climate and for human health

- Greenhouse gas (GHG) emissions are growing worldwide but they have been declining in almost all OECD countries between 2000 and 2012, revealing an overall decoupling from economic growth. This is partly explained by the slowdown in economic activity following the economic crisis, but also by the strengthening of climate policies and changing pattern of energy consumption.
- OECD countries however emit far more carbon dioxide (CO_2) per capita than most other world regions, with 9.6 tonnes per person compared with 3.4 tonnes per person in the rest of the world. With current policies, global emissions of CO_2 are estimated to reach about three times more than what would be required to limit the long-term increase in global temperatures to 2 °C.
- Sulphur oxide (SO_X) and nitrogen oxide (NO_X) emissions continue their downward trend as a result of energy savings, fuel substitution, pollution control and technical progress.
- In half of the OECD countries, over 90% of the population is exposed to concentrations of fine particulates ($PM_{2.5}$) above which adverse health effects have been observed. These particulates penetrate deep in the lungs and may include heavy metals and toxic organic substances.

Water demand is increasing but water use remained stable

- Freshwater abstractions remained stable due to more efficient use and better pricing policies, but also to greater exploitation of alternative water sources such as re-used and desalinated water. While many countries show a relative decoupling of water abstractions from GDP growth, in a third of countries, freshwater resources are under medium to high stress, and many countries have to cope with local or seasonal water shortages. Climate change may further exacerbate such shortages, including in countries that benefit from a reliable water supply.
- Close to 80% of the population of OECD countries benefit from wastewater treatment. Several countries now face increasing costs to upgrade ageing water supply and sanitation networks. Some have to find other ways of serving small or isolated settlements and ensuring proper control of small independent treatment facilities.

Landfill remains the major disposal method for municipal waste

- The generation of municipal waste slowed down in the 2000s. A person living in the OECD area generates on average 520 kg of waste per year; this is 30 kg less than in 2000, though still 20 kg more than in 1990. While waste is increasingly fed back into the economy through recycling, landfill remains the major disposal method in half of the OECD countries.

Threats to biodiversity are increasing

- Many animal and plant species in OECD countries are endangered, particularly in countries with a high population and infrastructure density. In North America and Europe, farmland and forest birds have declined by nearly 30% in 40 years. Many forests are threatened by degradation, fragmentation and conversion to other uses. Demand for wood to reach renewable energy targets plays a growing role in the exploitation of forests.

Environmental progress in economic sectors in uneven

- Energy intensity continued to improve over the 2000-14 period. Renewable energy is increasingly used, particularly in Europe. Renewables account for 21% of OECD electricity production (15.6% in 2000), and for almost 9% of total supply (6% in 2000). But fossil fuels still dominate supply (80%).
- In most OECD countries, road traffic growth rates exceeded economic growth. Countries' efforts to promote cleaner vehicles are often offset by increases in vehicle stocks and traffic, resulting in additional fuel consumption and pollution.
- Farmland decreased in nearly all countries as did some agriculture-related GHG emissions and the use of phosphate fertilisers. However, the share of land under organic farming remains low, just above 2%, though this masks substantial variations across countries. The shares tend to be higher in the European Union, reaching 10% to 17% in some countries.

Support to research, development and innovation is growing

- Public R&D spending dedicated to environment grew by more than 20% since 2000, and recovered at a faster rate than total public R&D after the 2008 economic crisis. Its share in total public R&D spending represents however less than 2%. The share of spending on renewable energy in total energy spending increased from 8% to 24%.

- Official development aid (ODA) for environmental purposes continued to rise; its share in total ODA increased from 9.6% in 2002 to 12.6%, aid for renewable energy surpassed aid for non-renewables.

Implementing market instruments to price pollution remains difficult

- The use of environmentally related taxes is growing but remains limited compared to labour taxes. The revenue they raised represented about 1.6% of GDP in 2013. It is dominated by taxes on energy (69%) and on motor vehicles and transport (28%). Variations in energy tax rates, uneven price signals, low levels of taxation on fuels with high environmental impacts, and exemptions for fuel used in some sectors impede the transition to a low-carbon economy. Many countries still apply higher taxes for petrol than for diesel, and the share of taxes in end-use prices is generally higher for households than for industry.

Reader's guide

Environment at a Glance presents selected environmental indicators. The report shows the progress that OECD countries have made since 2000 in addressing a range of environmental challenges. These include air and water pollution, climate change, waste management, and the protection of biodiversity and other natural assets.

They build on data provided regularly by member countries' authorities using an OECD questionnaire, and on data available from other OECD and international sources. Some indicators were updated on the basis of international information available in March 2015 and on the basis of comments from national Delegates received by February 2015. Nevertheless, due to delays in the production of environmental data in most countries, the most recent data for many of the parameters examined in this report is 2012.

The indicators in this report are those that are regularly used in the OECD's work and for which data are available for a majority of OECD countries.

Framework of OECD work on environmental data and indicators

For more than 30 years, the OECD has prepared harmonised international data and sets of indicators on the environment, assisted countries to improve their environmental information systems. The main aims of this work have been:

- to measure environmental progress and performance;
- to monitor and promote policy integration, in particular, the integration of environmental considerations into policy sectors, such as transport, energy and agriculture, and into economic policies more broadly;
- to help monitor progress towards sustainable development and green growth by measuring the extent of decoupling of environmental pressure from economic growth.

The OECD approach to indicators is based on the view that:

- There is no unique set of indicators; whether a given set of indicators is appropriate depends on its use.
- Indicators are only one tool among others and generally should be used with other information in order to draw robust conclusions.
- OECD environmental indicators are relatively small sets of indicators that have been identified for use at the international level, and should be complemented by national indicators when examining issues at national level.

The programme builds on agreement by OECD member countries:

- to use the pressure-state-response (PSR) model as a common reference framework;
- to identify indicators on the basis of their policy relevance, analytical soundness and measurability;
- to use the OECD approach and adapt it to their national circumstances.

The development of environmental indicators in OECD has been grounded in the practical experience of OECD countries. Their development has benefited from strong support from member countries, and their representatives in the OECD Working Party on Environmental Information. OECD work on indicators also benefits from close cooperation with other international organisations, notably the United Nations Statistics Division (UNSD) and United Nations regional offices, the United Nations Environment programme (UNEP), the World Bank, the European Union (including Eurostat and the European Environment Agency), as well as international institutes.

The OECD Pressure-State-Response model

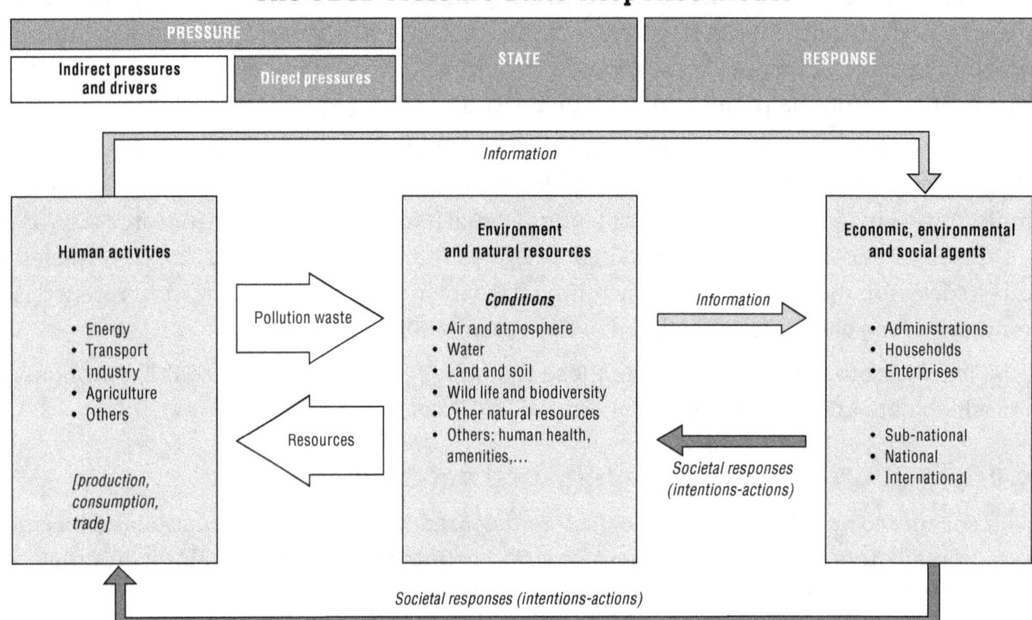

Comparability and interpretation

Each indicator presented in the report is preceded by a short text that explains in general terms what is measured and why, and by a description of the concept and definitions underlying the indicator. This is followed by a brief description of the main trends that can be observed. A paragraph on comparability highlights those areas where some caution may be needed when comparing indicators across countries or over time. Issues that cut across the subject areas are described below. An Annex provides additional information and country notes.

The indicators presented here are of varying relevance for different countries and should be interpreted taking account of the context in which they were produced. It should be borne in mind that national averages can mask significant variations *within* countries. In addition, care should be taken when making international comparisons:

- Definitions and measurement methods vary among countries, hence inter-country comparisons may not compare the same things.
- There is a level of uncertainty associated with the data sources and measurement methods on which the indicators rely. Differences between two countries' indicators are thus not always statistically significant; and when countries are clustered around a relatively narrow range of outcomes, it may be misleading to establish an order of ranking.

No single approach has been used for normalising the indicators; different denominators are used in parallel to balance the message conveyed. Many of the indicators shown in this publication are expressed on a per capita and per unit of GDP basis.

- The population estimates used are based on the SNA notion of residency: namely they include persons who are resident in a country for one year or more, regardless of their citizenship. The data generally refer to mid-year estimates, and come from the OECD Labour Force Statistics (ALFS) (OECD, 2014), "Population projections", OECD *Historical Population Data and Projections Statistics* (database), *http://dx.doi.org/10.1787/lfs-lfs-data-en*.
- The GDP figures used are expressed in USD and in 2005 prices and purchasing power parities (PPPs). PPPs are the rates of currency conversion that equalise the purchasing power of different countries by eliminating differences in price levels between countries. When converted by means of PPPs, expenditures on GDP across countries are expressed at the same set of prices, enabling comparisons between countries that reflect only differences in the volume of goods and services purchased.
- The data for OECD countries come from the *OECD National Accounts Statistics* (database), *http://dx.doi.org/10.1787/na-ana-data-en*, and from the *OECD Economic Outlook* (OECD, 2014) "OECD Economic Outlook No. 95", *OECD Economic Outlook: Statistics and Projections* (database), *http://dx.doi.org/10.1787/data-00688-en*. The data for the world and the BRIICS come from the World Bank ("World Bank Open Data", The World Bank, Washington, DC, *http://data.worldbank.org*).

Online data

A database with selected environmental data and indicators is available online and contains longer time series than the publication: *http://dx.doi/10.1787/env-data-en*. The following is a list of the datasets which are available:

- Greenhouse gas emissions by source: *http://dx.doi.org/10.1787/data-00594-en*.
- Air emissions by source: *http://dx.doi.org/10.1787/data-00598-en*.
- Air and greenhouse gas emissions by industry: *http://dx.doi.org/10.1787/data-00735-en*.
- CO_2 emissions from fuel combustion: *http://dx.doi.org/10.1787/co2-data-en*.
- Threatened species: *http://dx.doi.org/10.1787/data-00605-en*.
- Forest resources: *http://dx.doi.org/10.1787/data-00600-en*.
- Municipal waste: *http://dx.doi.org/10.1787/data-00601-en*.
- Freshwater abstractions: *http://dx.doi.org/10.1787/data-00602-en*.
- Freshwater resources: *http://dx.doi.org/10.1787/data-00603-en*.
- Wastewater treatment: *http://dx.doi.org/10.1787/data-00604-en*.
- Environmentally related taxes: *http://dx.doi.org/10.1787/data-00696-en*.

Websites

- OECD Environmental Data and Indicators: *www.oecd.org/env/indicators*.
- OECD Environmental Indicators, Country Profiles: *www.oecd.org/site/envind*.

Further reading

Useful references for "further reading" are available at the bottom of most sections.

For all sections, additional information can be found in:

- OECD (2014), "Green Growth Indicators 2014", *OECD Green Growth Studies*, OECD Publishing, Paris, *http://dx.doi.org/10.1787/9789264202030-en.*
- OECD (2014), *OECD Factbook 2014: Economic, Environmental and Social Statistics*, OECD Publishing, Paris, *http://dx.doi.org/10.1787/factbook-2014-en.*
- OECD (2012), *OECD Environmental Outlook to 2050: The Consequences of Inaction*, OECD Publishing, Paris, *http://dx.doi.org/10.1787/9789264122246-en.*

Acronyms and abbreviations

Signs

The following signs are used in figures and tables:

..: not available.

0: nil or negligible.

.: decimal point.

x: not applicable.

Country aggregates

OECD America	This zone includes the following member countries of the OECD: Canada, Chile,[1] Mexico and the United States.
OECD Europe	This zone includes all European member countries of the OECD, i.e. Austria, Belgium, the Czech Republic, Denmark, Estonia,[1] Finland, France, Germany, Greece, Hungary, Iceland, Ireland, Italy, Luxembourg, the Netherlands, Norway, Poland, Portugal, the Slovak Republic, Slovenia,[1] Spain, Sweden, Switzerland, Turkey and the United Kingdom.
OECD Asia-Oceania	This zone includes the following member countries of the OECD: Australia, Israel,[1] Japan, Korea and New Zealand.
OECD	This zone includes all member countries of the OECD, i.e. countries of OECD America plus countries of OECD Asia-Oceania and countries of OECD Europe.
BRIICS	Brazil, Russian Federation, India, Indonesia, People's Republic of China, South Africa.

Country aggregates may include Secretariat estimates.

1. Chile has been a member of the OECD since 7 May 2010, Slovenia since 21 July 2010, Estonia since 9 December 2010 and Israel since 7 September 2010.

Country codes

AUS	Australia	FRA	France	NLD	Netherlands
AUT	Austria	GBR	United Kingdom	NZL	New Zealand
BEL	Belgium	GRC	Greece	NOR	Norway
CAN	Canada	HUN	Hungary	POL	Poland
CHE	Switzerland	ISL	Iceland	PRT	Portugal
CHL	Chile	IRL	Ireland	SVK	Slovak Republic
CZE	Czech Republic	ITA	Italy	SVN	Slovenia
DEU	Germany	ISR	Israel	SWE	Sweden
DNK	Denmark	JPN	Japan	TUR	Turkey
ESP	Spain	KOR	Korea	USA	United States
EST	Estonia	LUX	Luxembourg		
FIN	Finland	MEX	Mexico	EU	European Union

Abbreviations

BOD	Biochemical oxygen demand
cap	Capita
CDDA	Common database on designated areas, EEA
CFCs	Chlorofluorocarbons
CH_4	Methane

CO_2	Carbon dioxide
CO_2 eq	Carbon dioxide equivalent
COD	Chemical oxygen demand
DAC	Development Assistance Committee, OECD
EEA	European Environment Agency
EMEP	European Monitoring and Evaluation Programme
FAO	The United Nations Food and Agriculture Organization
GBAORD	Government budget appropriations on R&D
GDP	Gross domestic product
GHG	Greenhouse gas
GNI	Gross national income
ha	Hectare
HFCs	Hydrofluorocarbons
ICES	International Council for the Exploration of the Sea
IEA	International Energy Agency
IPCC	Intergovernmental Panel on Climate Change
ISIC	International Standard Industrial Classification
IUCN	International Union for Conservation of Nature
Mt	Million tonnes
Mtoe	Million tonnes of oil equivalent
m^3	Cubic meter
N	Nitrogen
NO_X	Nitrogen oxides
NO_2	Nitrogen dioxide
N_2O	Nitrous oxide
ODA	Official development assistance
P	Phosphorous
PFC	Perfluorocarbons
PM	Particulate matter
$PM_{2.5}$	Fine particulate matter, smaller than 2.5 microns in diameter
PM_{10}	Small particulate matter, smaller than 10 microns in diameter
PPP	Purchasing power parities
RSPB	Royal Society for the protection of birds
SF_6	Sulphur hexafluoride
SO_x	Sulphur oxides
SO_2	Sulphur dioxide
t	Tonne
TEEB	The economics of ecosystems and biodiversity
TPES	Total primary energy supply
toe	Tonne of oil equivalent
µg	microgram
UNECE	UN Economic Commission for Europe
UNEP	UN Environment Programme
UNFCCC	UN Framework Convention on Climate Change
UNSD	UN Statistics Division
USD	US dollar
WCMC	World Conservation Monitoring Centre, UNEP
WDPA	World database on protected areas, UNEP
WHO	World Health Organization
WMO	World Meteorological Organization
WWAP	UN World Water Assessment Programme

1. ENVIRONMENTAL TRENDS

Greenhouse gas (GHG) emissions

Carbon dioxide (CO_2) emissions

Sulphur oxides (SO_X) and nitrogen oxides (NO_X) emissions

Particulate emissions and population exposure

Use of freshwater resources

Water pricing for public supply

Wastewater treatment

Biological diversity

Use of forest resources

Use of fish resources

Municipal waste

Greenhouse gas (GHG) emissions

Emissions of greenhouses gases (GHGs) from human activities disturb the radiative energy balance of the earth-atmosphere system. They exacerbate the natural greenhouse effect, leading to temperature changes and other consequences for the earth's climate. Land use changes and forestry also play a role by altering the amount of greenhouse gases captured or released by carbon sinks.

Climate change is of concern mainly as regards its impact on ecosystems (biodiversity), human settlements and agriculture, and on the frequency and scale of extreme weather events. It could have significant consequences for human well-being and socio-economic activities, which could in turn affect global economic output.

Definitions

The indicators presented here refer to the sum of emissions of six GHGs that have direct effects on climate change and are considered responsible for a major part of global warming: carbon dioxide (CO_2), methane (CH_4), nitrous oxide (N_2O), chlorofluorocarbons (CFCs), hydrofluorocarbons (HFCs), perfluorocarbons (PFCs) and sulphur hexafluoride (SF_6).

They show gross emissions expressed in CO_2 equivalents as well as emission intensities per unit of GDP and per capita, and related changes. They refer to GHGs emitted within the national territory and exclude CO_2 emissions and removals from land use change and forestry. They do not cover international transactions of emission reduction units or certified emission reductions.

These indicators should be read in conjunction with indicators on CO_2 emissions, energy intensity, and energy prices and taxes. Their interpretation should take into account the structure of countries' energy supply and climatic factors.

Overview

Global GHG emissions have doubled since the early 1970s, driven by economic growth and increasing fossil energy use in developing countries. Historically, OECD countries emitted the bulk of global GHGs, but the share of the BRIICS in global emissions has been increasing to over 40%. CO_2 determines the overall trend. Together with CH_4 and N_2O, it accounts for about 98% of GHG emissions.

Emissions have been declining in recent years in almost all OECD countries. They fell by almost 5% since 2008 in the OECD area. This is partly due to a slowdown in economic activity following the 2008 economic crisis, but also to a strengthening of climate policies and changing patterns of energy consumption. As a result, emission intensities per unit of GDP and per capita decreased between 2000 and 2012 in almost all OECD countries, revealing a strong overall decoupling from economic growth.

Reductions in national emissions may also be the result of offshoring domestic production and the associated emissions. Evidence of decoupling based on domestic emissions per unit of GDP or per capita, therefore, may reveal only part of the story.

Individual OECD countries' rates of progress vary significantly. This partly reflects different national circumstances, such as composition and rate of economic growth, population growth, energy resource endowment, and the extent to which the countries have taken steps to reduce emissions from various sources. Today, emissions per capita range from 6 to 24 tonnes per inhabitant, and the related change since 2000 ranges from +32% to -29%.

Comparability

Data on GHG emissions are reported annually to the Secretariat of the UNFCCC with 1990 as a base year but not by all OECD countries. They display a good level of comparability. The high per-GDP emissions of Estonia result from the use of oil shale for electricity generation. Oil shale has a high carbon emission factor. The high per-capita emissions of Luxembourg result from the lower taxation of road fuels compared to neighbouring countries, which attracts drivers to refuel in the country.

Latest year available: years prior to 2009 were not considered. The OECD totals do not include Israel.

For additional notes, see the Annex.

Sources

OECD (2014), "Greenhouse gas Emissions by Source", *OECD Environment Statistics* (database), *http://dx.doi.org/10.1787/data-00594-en*.

Further information

OECD (2015), *Aligning Policies for a Low-Carbon Economy*, OECD Publishing, Paris, *http://dx.doi.org/10.1787/9789264233294-en*.

OECD (2012), *OECD Environmental Outlook to 2050: The Consequences of Inaction*, OECD Publishing, Paris, *http://dx.doi.org/10.1787/9789264122246-en*.

UNFCCC (2014), Greenhouse Gas Inventory Data, *http://unfccc.int/ghg_data/items/3800.php*.

Information on data for Israel: *http://dx.doi.org/10.1787/888932315602*.

Figure 1.1. **Greenhouse gas emission intensities per capita, 2012**

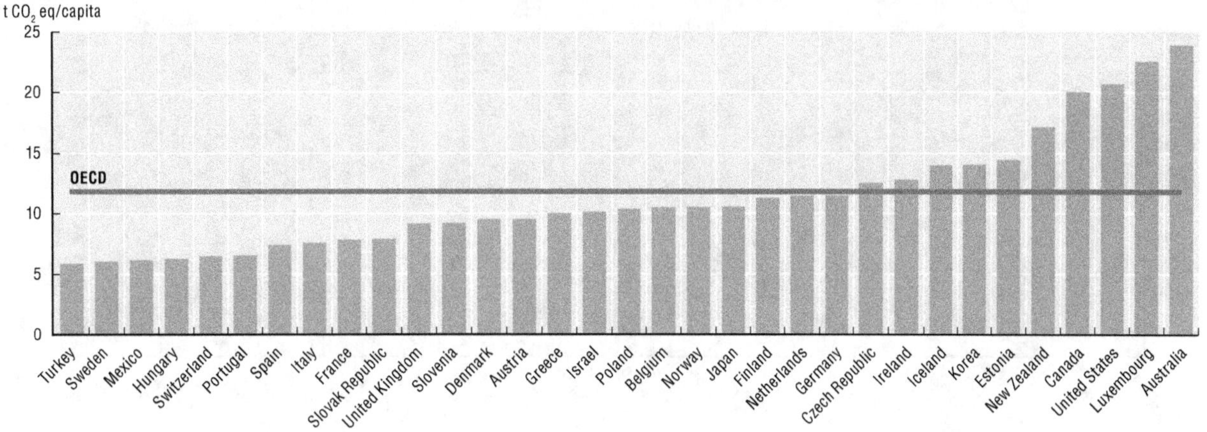

Source: OECD (2014), "Greenhouse gas Emissions by Source", *OECD Environment Statistics* (database); UNFCCC (2014), Greenhouse Gas Inventory Data.

StatLink http://dx.doi.org/10.1787/888933261683

Table 1.1. **Greenhouse gas emissions and intensities**

	Total GHG emissions			Emission intensities				GDP
	Million tonnes CO_2 eq.	% change		Per unit of GDP		Per capita		% change
	2012	1990-2012	2000-12	t/1 000 USD 2012	% change 2000-12	t/cap 2012	% change 2000-12	2000-12
Australia	544	31	11	0.62	-23	24	-7	44
Austria	80	3	0	0.25	-17	10	-5	21
Belgium	117	-18	-20	0.31	-32	10	-26	18
Canada	699	18	-3	0.54	-24	20	-15	27
Chile	..	..	..	..	..	..	..	68
Czech Republic	131	-33	-10	0.51	-35	13	-12	38
Denmark	53	-24	-24	0.29	-29	9	-28	8
Estonia	19	-53	12	0.77	-29	14	16	58
Finland	61	-13	-12	0.34	-26	11	-16	20
France	496	-11	-12	0.24	-24	8	-18	16
Germany	939	-25	-10	0.32	-21	11	-9	14
Greece	111	6	-12	0.47	-14	10	-14	1
Hungary	62	-36	-19	0.36	-34	6	-17	22
Iceland	4	26	14	0.38	-15	14	1	35
Ireland	59	6	-14	0.34	-34	13	-29	31
Israel	78	..	8	0.35	-25	10	-12	49
Italy	460	-11	-17	0.28	-17	8	-22	1
Japan	1 343	9	0	0.34	-8	11	0	9
Korea	698	136	36	0.47	-15	14	29	63
Luxembourg	12	-8	21	0.33	-9	23	1	33
Mexico	701	53	24	0.48	3	6	10	30
Netherlands	192	-10	-10	0.29	-21	11	-14	15
New Zealand	76	25	7	0.65	-21	17	-7	35
Norway	53	5	-2	0.22	-19	11	-13	21
Poland	399	-14	1	0.56	-36	10	0	56
Portugal	69	13	-18	0.30	-20	7	-20	2
Slovak Republic	43	-42	-13	0.37	-48	8	-13	67
Slovenia	19	3	0	0.37	-22	9	-4	27
Spain	341	20	-10	0.27	-26	7	-22	21
Sweden	58	-21	-16	0.17	-33	6	-22	26
Switzerland	51	-3	-1	0.15	-20	6	-10	24
Turkey	440	133	48	0.43	-9	6	32	62
United Kingdom	584	-25	-16	0.27	-31	9	-22	21
United States	6 488	4	-8	0.46	-25	21	-18	22
OECD	**15 506**	**5**	**-4**	**0.39**	**-21**	**12**	**-11**	**22**
OECD America	8 000	10	-5	0.46	-23	17	-15	24
OECD Asia-Oceania	2 654	30	10	0.41	-11	13	6	24
OECD Europe	4 853	-11	-8	0.31	-23	9	-13	19

Note: See the Annex for country notes.

Source: OECD (2014), "Greenhouse Gas Emissions by Source", *OECD Environment Statistics* (database); UNFCCC (2014), Greenhouse Gas Inventory Data.

StatLink http://dx.doi.org/10.1787/888933262258

Figure 1.2. **Greenhouse gas emissions, by gas, 2012**

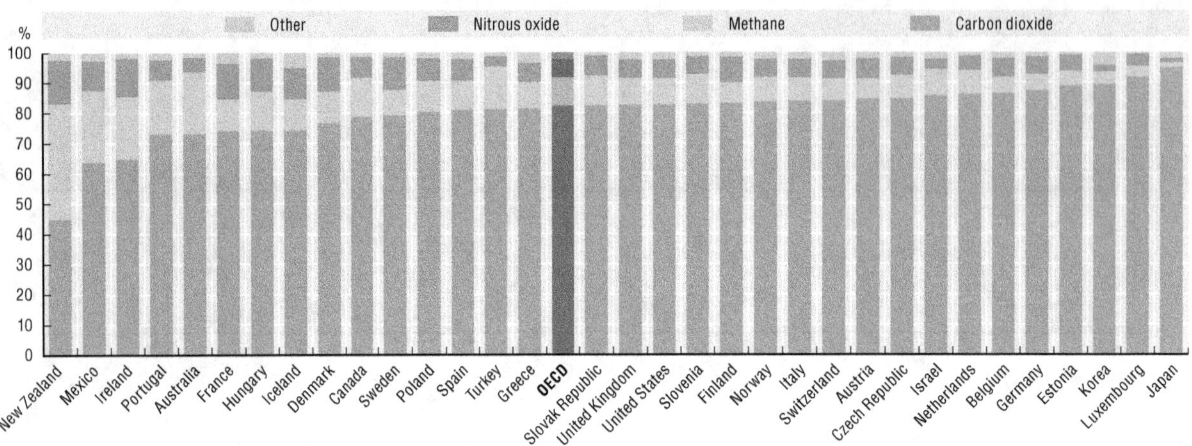

Source: OECD (2014), "Greenhouse Gas Emissions by Source", *OECD Environment Statistics* (database); UNFCCC (2014), Greenhouse Gas Inventory Data.

StatLink http://dx.doi.org/10.1787/888933261690

Figure 1.3. **Greenhouse gas emission levels**

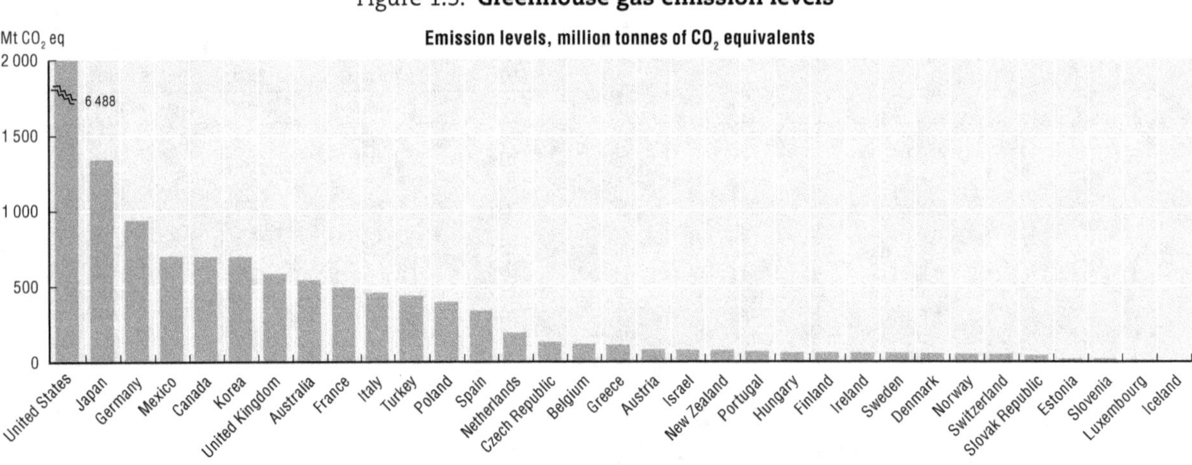

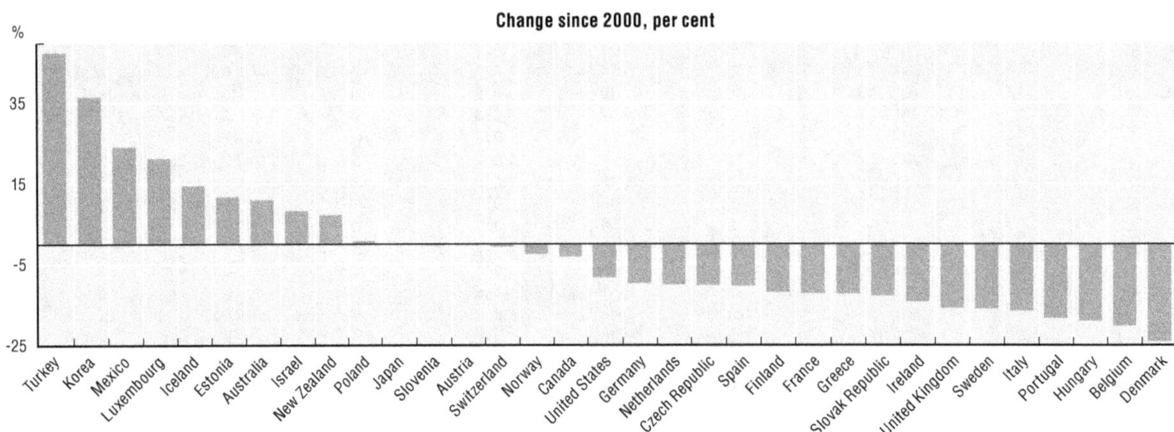

Source: OECD (2014), "Greenhouse Gas Emissions by Source", *OECD Environment Statistics* (database); UNFCCC (2014), Greenhouse Gas Inventory Data.

StatLink http://dx.doi.org/10.1787/888933261700

Figure 1.4. **Greenhouse gas emission intensities per GDP, 2012**

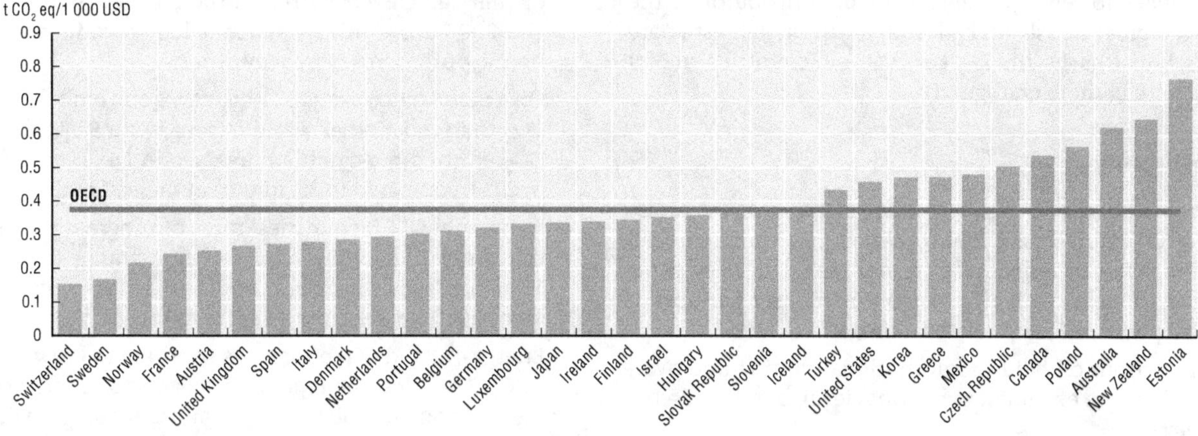

Source: OECD (2014), "Greenhouse Gas Emissions by Source", *OECD Environment Statistics* (database); UNFCCC (2014), Greenhouse Gas Inventory Data.

StatLink http://dx.doi.org/10.1787/888933261713

Figure 1.5. **Change in greenhouse gas emission intensities, since 2000**

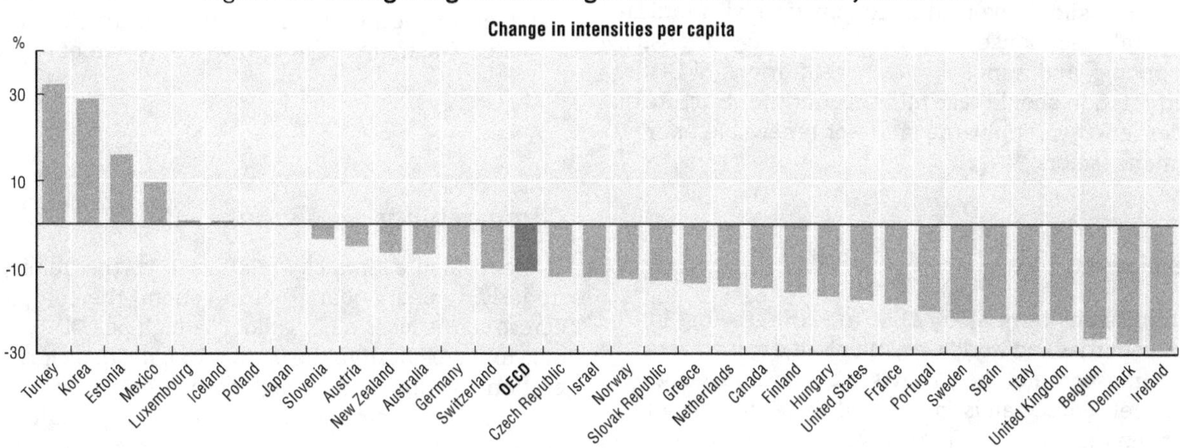

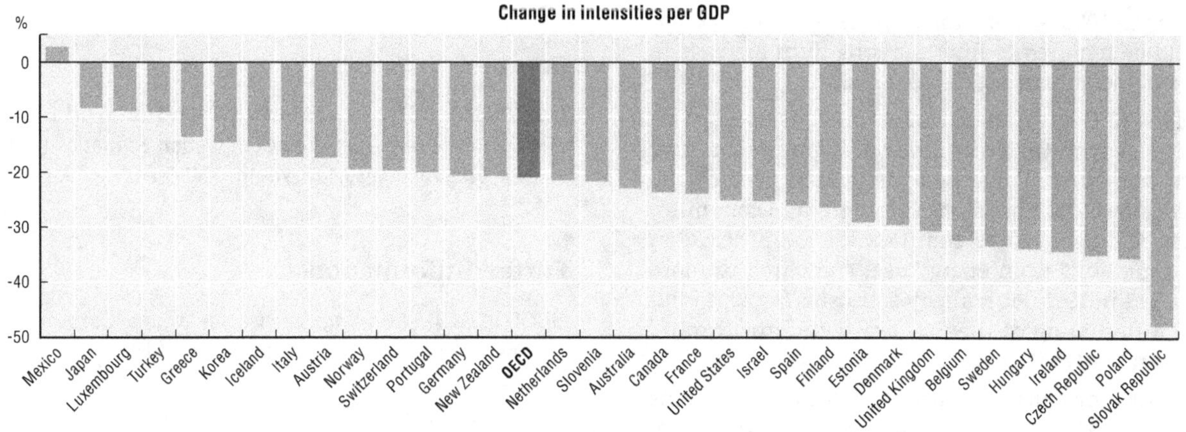

Source: OECD (2014), "Greenhouse Gas Emissions by Source", *OECD Environment Statistics* (database); UNFCCC (2014), Greenhouse Gas Inventory Data.

StatLink http://dx.doi.org/10.1787/888933261723

Carbon dioxide (CO_2) emissions

Carbon dioxide (CO_2) from the combustion of fossil fuels and biomass for energy use is a major contributor to the enhanced greenhouse effect. It makes up the largest share of greenhouse gases and is a key factor in countries' ability to deal with climate change.

Definitions

The indicators presented here refer to gross direct emissions of CO_2 from fossil fuel combustion. Human-caused emissions from other sources are not included. They show total emissions as well as emission intensities per unit of GDP and per capita, and related changes.

Emissions from oil held in international marine and aviation bunkers are excluded at national level, but included at world level.

CO_2 removal by sinks, indirect emissions from land use changes and indirect effects through interactions in the atmosphere are not taken into account.

This indicator should be read in conjunction with indicators on total greenhouse gas emissions, energy intensity, energy pricing, and atmospheric concentrations of GHGs. Its interpretation should take into account the structure of countries' energy supply, the share of renewable energy, and climatic factors.

Overview

CO_2 emissions from energy use are still growing in many countries and worldwide, mainly due to increases in the transport and the energy sectors. In 2013, global energy-related CO_2 emissions reached a record high of 32.2 billion tonnes, and in 2010 accounted for around 75% of global GHG emissions. With current policies, these emissions are estimated to exceed 50 billion tonnes in 2050 – about three times more than what would be required to limit the long-term increase in global temperatures to 2 degree Celsius.

Since 1990, energy-related CO_2 emissions have grown more slowly in OECD countries as a group than they have worldwide. This trend was emphasised by the rapid growth of emissions in emerging economies. Today, OECD countries emit less than 40% of global CO_2 emissions from energy use, compared to more than 50% in 1990. Preliminary estimates for 2014 indicate a flattening of the CO_2 emission growth rate, independently of economic growth.

Since 2000, overall OECD energy-related CO_2 emissions have decreased or grown at a slower rate than economic growth. This is due to structural changes in industry and energy supply and improvements in energy efficiency in production processes. In more than half of OECD countries, emissions have decreased since 2000, displaying an absolute decoupling. Most of this decrease occurred in the late 2000s following the 2008 economic crisis that led to reduced economic output in several countries.

On a per-capita basis, OECD countries still emit far more CO_2 than most other world regions, with 9.6 tonnes of CO_2 emitted per capita on average in OECD countries in 2013, compared to 3.4 tonnes in the rest of the world.

Individual OECD countries' rates of progress vary significantly. Today, emissions per capita range from 4 to 18 tonnes per person, and the related change since 2000 ranges from +48% to -33%.

Energy-related CO_2 emissions continue to grow in the OECD Asia-Oceania region. This is due to energy supply and consumption patterns and trends, often combined with relatively low energy prices.

Reductions in national emissions can also be achieved by offshoring domestic production and, thus, the related emissions. Evidence of decoupling based on domestic emissions per unit of GDP or per capita, therefore, may reveal only part of the story.

Comparability

The emission estimates are affected by the quality of the underlying energy data, but in general the comparability across countries is quite good. The high per-GDP emissions of Estonia result from the use of oil shale for electricity generation. Oil shale has a high carbon emission factor. The high per-capita emissions of Luxembourg result from the lower taxation of road fuels compared to neighbouring countries, which attracts drivers to refuel in the country.

Sources

IEA (2015), "CO_2 Emissions by Product and Flow", *IEA CO_2 Emissions from Fuel Combustion Statistics* (database), *http://dx.doi.org/10.1787/data-00430-en.*

Further information

OECD (2015), *Aligning Policies for a Low-Carbon Economy*, OECD Publishing, Paris, *http://dx.doi.org/10.1787/9789264233294-en.*

OECD (2013), *OECD Regions at a Glance 2013*, OECD Publishing, Paris, *http://dx.doi.org/10.1787/reg_glance-2013-en.*

OECD (2012), *OECD Environmental Outlook to 2050: The Consequences of Inaction*, OECD Publishing, Paris, *http://dx.doi.org/10.1787/9789264122246-en.*

Information on data for Israel: *http://dx.doi.org/10.1787/888932315602.*

Figure 1.6. **CO_2 emission intensities per capita, 2013**

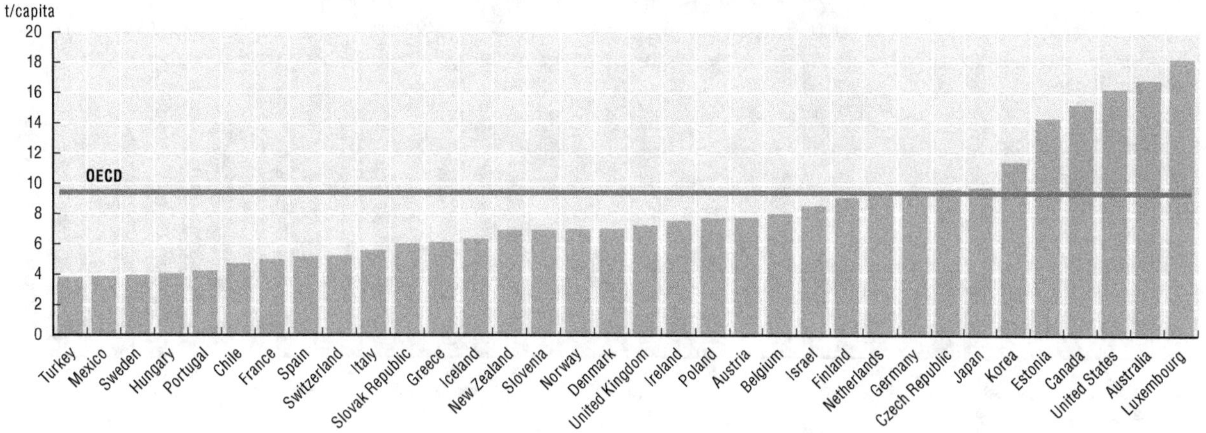

Source: IEA (2015), "CO_2 Emissions by Product and Flow", *IEA CO_2 Emissions from Fuel Combustion Statistics* (database).

StatLink http://dx.doi.org/10.1787/888933261734

Table 1.2. **CO_2 emissions and intensities**

	CO_2 emissions from energy use							GDP
	Total			Intensities per unit of GDP		Intensities per capita		
	Million tonnes	% change		t/1 000 USD	% change	t/cap	% change	% change
	2013	1990-2013	2000-13	2013	2000-13	2013	2000-13	2000-13
Australia	389	50	16	0.43	-21	17	-4	48
Austria	65	16	6	0.21	-13	8	0	21
Belgium	89	-16	-22	0.24	-34	8	-28	18
Canada	536	28	4	0.40	-20	15	-10	29
Chile	82	179	69	0.28	-3	5	48	74
Czech Republic	101	-33	-17	0.39	-39	10	-19	37
Denmark	39	-24	-24	0.21	-29	7	-27	7
Estonia	19	-48	30	0.74	-19	14	36	60
Finland	49	-8	-10	0.28	-23	9	-14	18
France	316	-9	-13	0.15	-25	5	-20	16
Germany	760	-19	-6	0.26	-18	9	-5	14
Greece	69	-1	-22	0.31	-20	6	-25	-3
Hungary	40	-40	-26	0.22	-40	4	-23	24
Iceland	2	7	-6	0.17	-33	6	-18	40
Ireland	34	14	-16	0.20	-36	7	-31	31
Israel	68	108	24	0.29	-19	8	-3	54
Italy	338	-13	-20	0.21	-19	6	-25	-1
Japan	1 235	18	7	0.30	-4	10	6	11
Korea	572	147	33	0.37	-21	11	24	68
Luxembourg	10	-9	21	0.27	-11	18	-2	36
Mexico	452	74	31	0.28	-0.3	4	12	32
Netherlands	156	8	-1	0.24	-13	9	-6	14
New Zealand	31	41	6	0.25	-23	7	-8	39
Norway	35	29	10	0.14	-9	7	-2	22
Poland	292	-15	1	0.41	-36	8	1	59
Portugal	45	19	-22	0.20	-23	4	-25	1
Slovak Republic	32	-41	-12	0.27	-48	6	-13	70
Slovenia	14	6	2	0.28	-19	7	-3	26
Spain	236	16	-15	0.19	-29	5	-26	20
Sweden	38	-28	-28	0.11	-43	4	-33	28
Switzerland	42	2	-1	0.12	-21	5	-11	26
Turkey	284	123	41	0.27	-17	4	25	69
United Kingdom	449	-18	-14	0.20	-30	7	-19	23
United States	5 120	7	-9	0.35	-27	16	-19	25
OECD	**12 038**	**9**	**-3**	**0.30**	**-22**	**10**	**-11**	**24**
OECD America	6 190	12	-6	0.35	-25	13	-17	27
OECD Asia-Oceania	2 295	44	14	0.33	-10	11	9	27
OECD Europe	3 553	-9	-9	0.23	-24	6	-14	20
World	**32 200**	**54**	**36**	**0.57**	**-2**	**4**	**16**	**39**

Note: See the Annex for country notes.
Source: IEA (2015), "CO_2 Emissions by Product and Flow", *IEA CO_2 Emissions from Fuel Combustion Statistics* (database).

StatLink http://dx.doi.org/10.1787/888933262261

Figure 1.7. **CO_2 emissions by source, 2013**

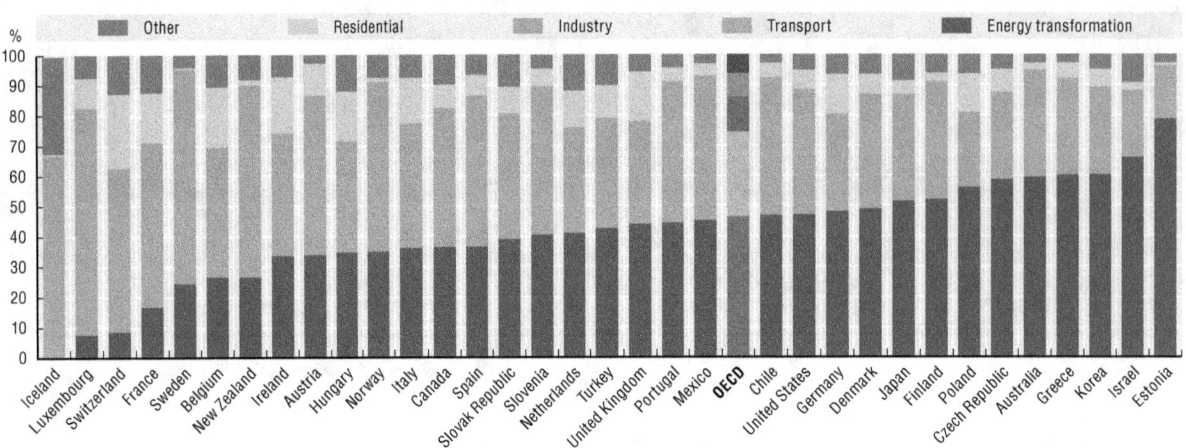

Source: IEA (2015), "CO_2 Emissions by Product and Flow", *IEA CO_2 Emissions from Fuel Combustion Statistics* (database).

StatLink http://dx.doi.org/10.1787/888933261746

Figure 1.8. **CO_2 emission levels**

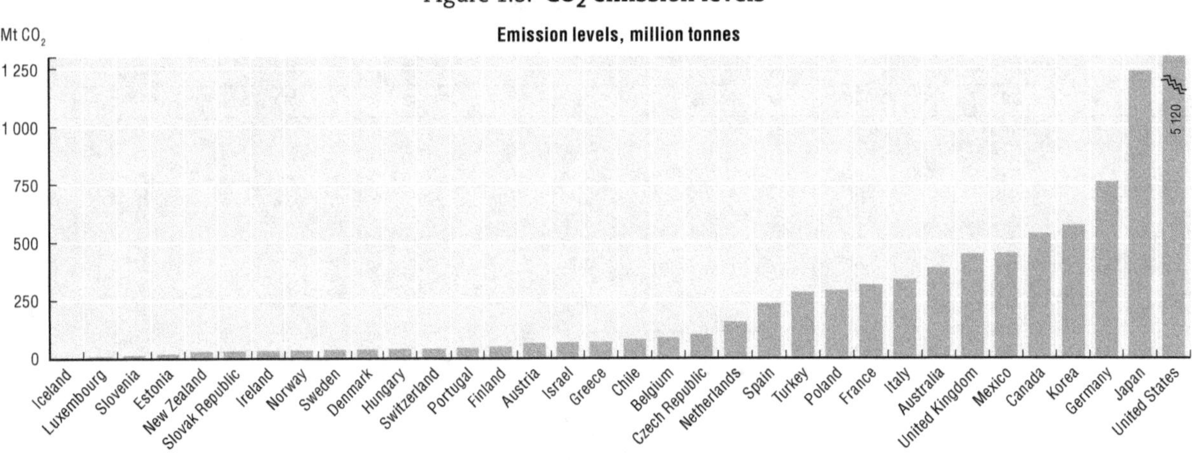

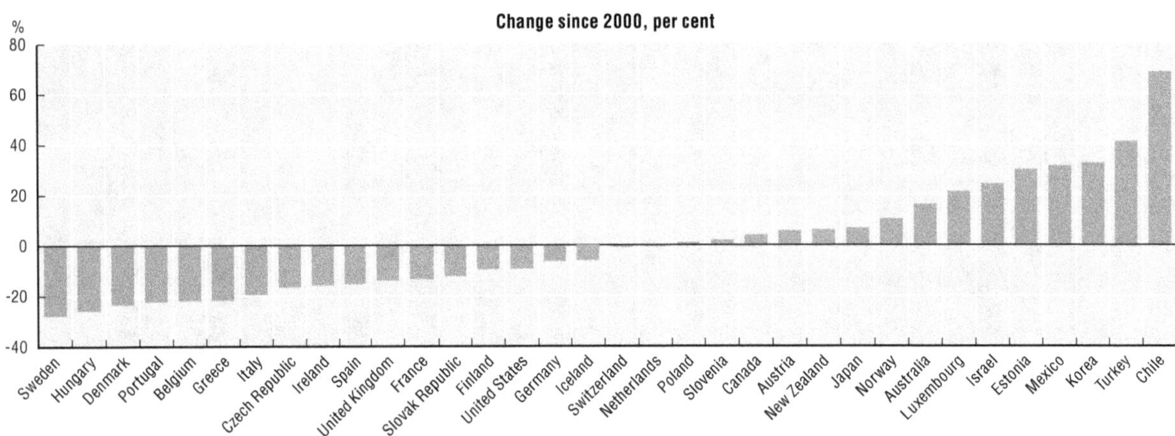

Source: IEA (2015), "CO_2 Emissions by Product and Flow", *IEA CO_2 Emissions from Fuel Combustion Statistics* (database).

StatLink http://dx.doi.org/10.1787/888933261750

Figure 1.9. **CO_2 emission intensities per GDP, 2013**

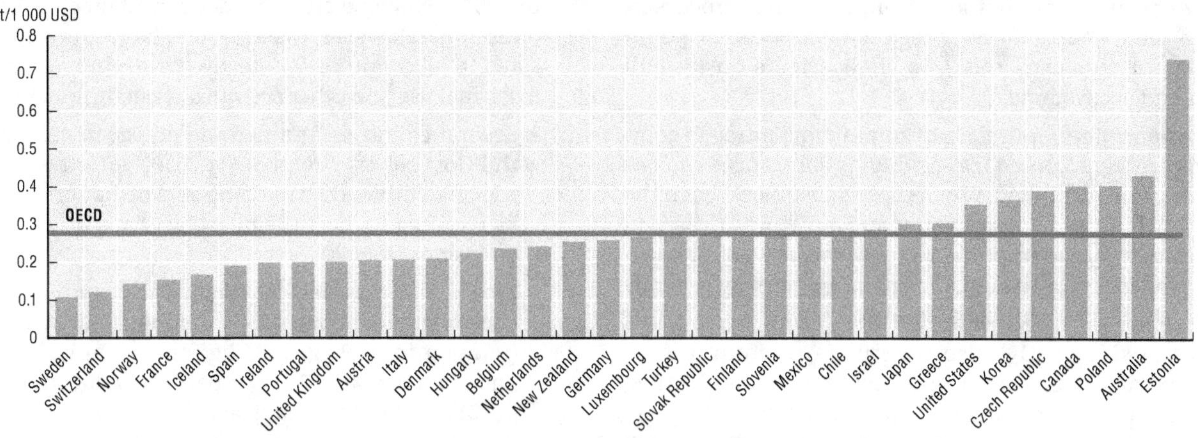

Source: IEA (2015), "CO_2 Emissions by Product and Flow", *IEA CO_2 Emissions from Fuel Combustion Statistics* (database).

StatLink http://dx.doi.org/10.1787/888933261763

Figure 1.10. **Change in CO_2 emission intensities, since 2000**

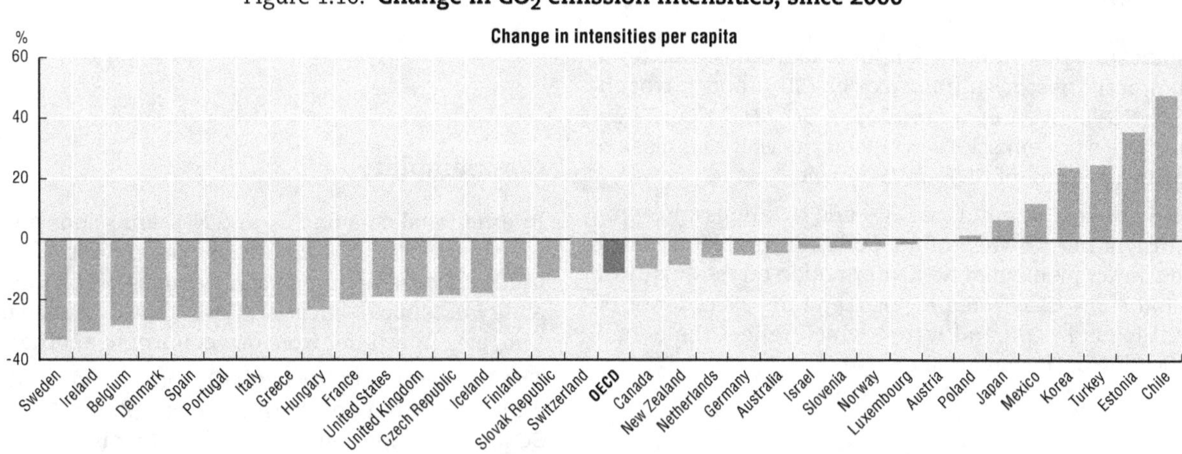

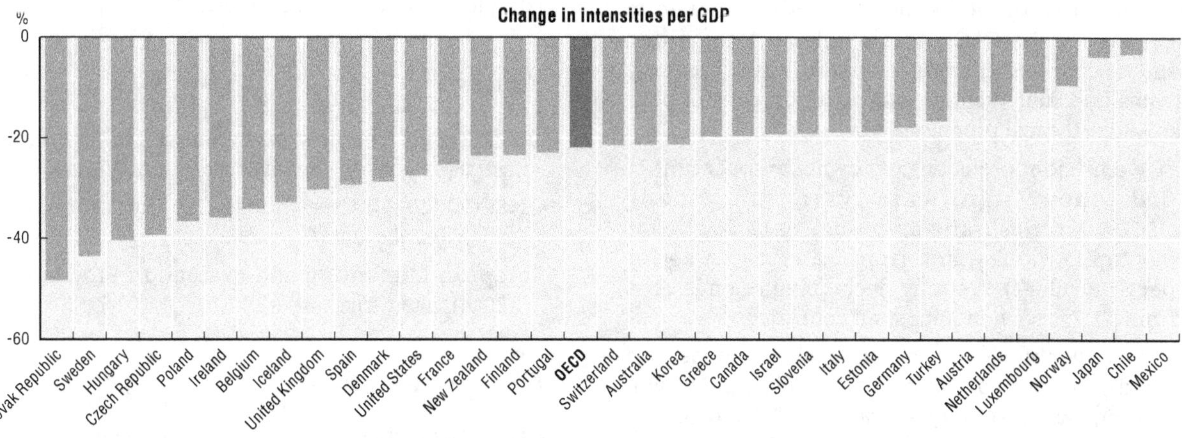

Source: IEA (2015), "CO_2 Emissions by Product and Flow", *IEA CO_2 Emissions from Fuel Combustion Statistics* (database).

StatLink http://dx.doi.org/10.1787/888933261770

Sulphur oxides (SO_X) and nitrogen oxides (NO_X) emissions

Atmospheric pollutants from energy transformation and energy consumption, but also from industrial processes, are the main contributors to regional and local air pollution. Major concerns relate to their effects on human health and ecosystems.

In the atmosphere, emissions of sulphur and nitrogen compounds are transformed into acidifying substances such as sulphuric and nitric acid. When these substances reach the ground, acidification of soil, water and buildings arises. Soil acidification is one important factor causing forest damage; acidification of the aquatic environment may severely impair the life of plant and animal species.

Nitrogen oxides (NO_X) also contribute to ground-level ozone formation and are responsible for eutrophication, reduction in water quality and species richness. They are associated with adverse effects on human health as high concentrations cause respiratory illnesses.

Definitions

The indicators presented here refer to total emissions from human activities of sulphur oxides (SO_X) and nitrogen oxides (NO_X), given as quantities of SO_2 and NO_2. They show changes in emissions over time, as well as emission intensities per unit of GDP and per capita.

It should be kept in mind that SO_X and NO_X emissions provide only a partial view of air pollution problems. They should be supplemented with information on the acidity of rain and snow in selected regions, and the exceedance of critical loads in soil and water, which reflect the actual acidification of the environment.

Overview

Compared to 2000, SO_X emissions have continued to decrease for the OECD as a whole as a combined result of changes in energy demand through energy savings and fuel substitution, pollution control policies and technical progress.

- SO_X emission intensities per capita and per unit of GDP show significant variation among OECD countries (ranging from 1 kg to 262 kg for per capita values, and from 0.1 kg to 7.1 kg for per GDP values). A strong decoupling of emissions from GDP is seen in almost all countries.
- The Gothenburg Protocol, adopted in Europe and North America to reduce acid precipitation even further, has been in force since May 2005. All countries reached the goal they fixed for 2010.

NO_X emissions have continued to decrease in the OECD overall since 2000, but less than SO_X emissions. This was mainly due to changes in energy demand, pollution control policies and technical progress. In the late 2000s, the slowdown in economic activity following the 2008 economic crisis further contributed to reduce emissions. However, these results have not compensated in all countries for steady growth in road traffic, fossil fuel use and other activities generating NO_X.

- Several countries attained the emission ceilings of the Gothenburg Protocol for 2010, but other countries had difficulties in doing so. Further efforts will be required to meet the new objectives for reducing emissions by 2020.
- Emission intensities per capita and per unit of GDP show significant variations among OECD countries (ranging from 9 kg to 86 kg for per capita values, and from 0.2 kg to 2 kg for per GDP values). Almost all OECD countries have achieved a strong decoupling from economic growth since the 2000.

Comparability

International data on SO_X and NO_X emissions are available for almost all OECD countries. The details of estimation methods for emissions such as emission factors and reliability, extent of sources and pollutants included in estimation, etc., may differ from one country to another.

The high emission levels of SO_X for Iceland are due to H_2S emissions from geothermal power plants (expressed as SO_2), which represented 80% of total emissions in 2012.

OECD totals do not include Chile and Mexico.

For additional notes, see the Annex.

Sources

OECD (2014), "Air Emissions by Source", *OECD Environment Statistics* (database), *http://dx.doi.org/10.1787/data-00598-en*.

UNFCCC (2014), Greenhouse Gas Inventory Data, *http://unfccc.int/ghg_data/items/3800.php*.

European Monitoring and Evaluation Programme (EMEP) (2014), *www.emep.int*.

Further information

OECD (2014), *The Cost of Air Pollution: Health Impacts of Road Transport*, OECD Publishing, Paris, *http://dx.doi.org/10.1787/9789264210448-en*.

UNECE (2014), "Convention on Long-Range Transboundary Air Pollution", *www.unece.org/env/lrtap/multi_h1.html*.

Information on data for Israel: *http://dx.doi.org/10.1787/888932315602*.

Figure 1.11. **Change in SO_X and NO_X emissions, since 2000**

Source: OECD (2014) "Air Emissions by Source", *OECD Environment Statistics* (database); European Monitoring and Evaluation Programme (EMEP) (2014); UNFCCC (2014), Greenhouse Gas Inventory Data.

StatLink http://dx.doi.org/10.1787/888933261786

Figure 1.12. **SO_X and NO_X emission intensities per unit of GDP, 2012 or latest available year**

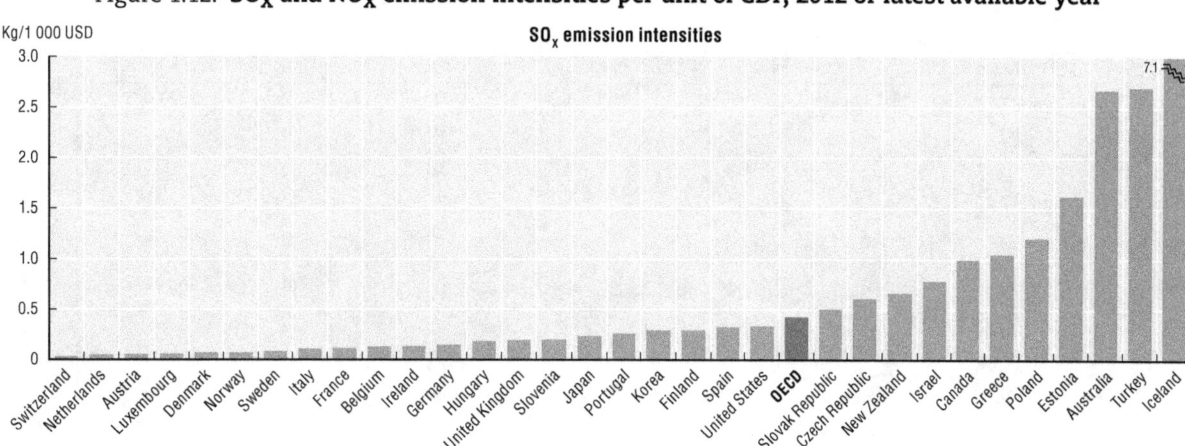
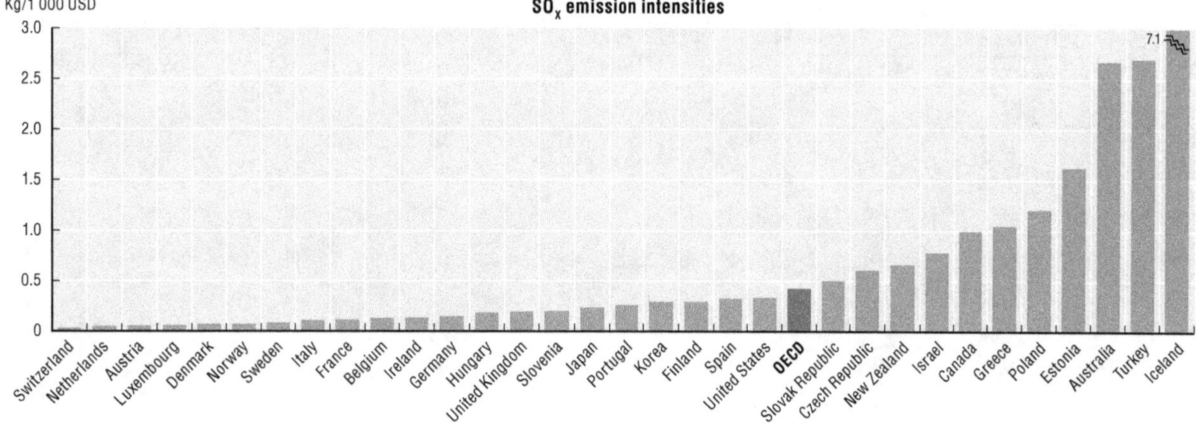

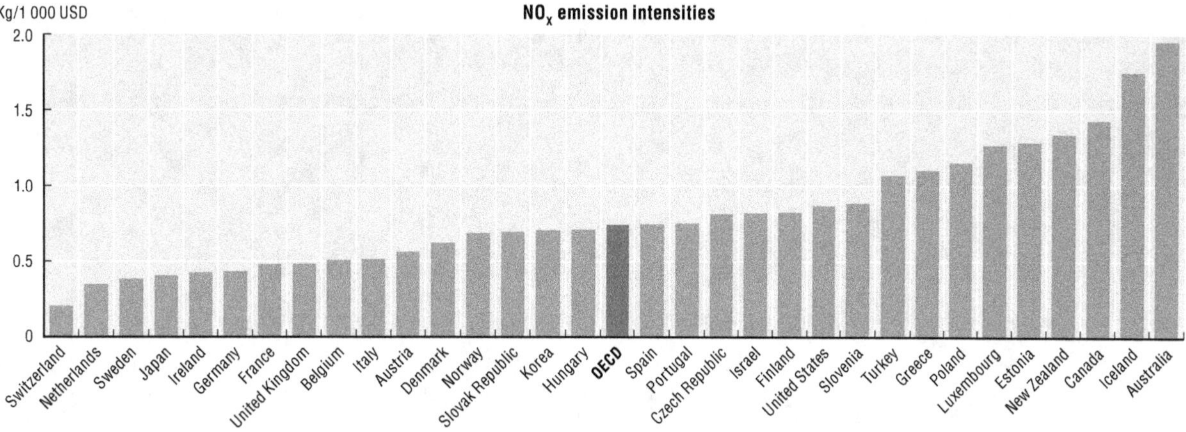

Source: OECD (2014) "Air Emissions by Source", *OECD Environment Statistics* (database); European Monitoring and Evaluation Programme (EMEP) (2014); UNFCCC (2014), Greenhouse Gas Inventory Data.

StatLink http://dx.doi.org/10.1787/888933261791

Figure 1.13. **SO_X emission intensities per capita, 2000, 2012**

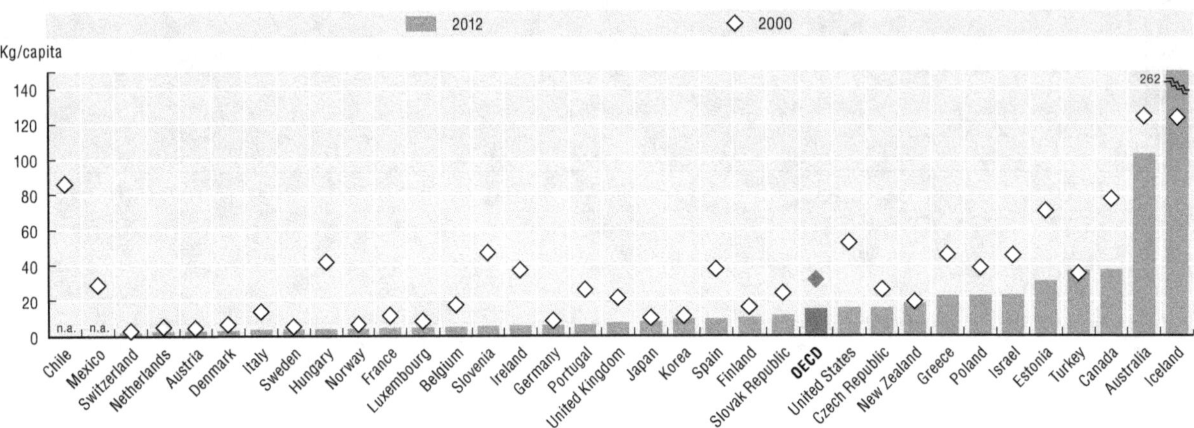

Source: OECD (2014) "Air Emissions by Source", *OECD Environment Statistics* (database); European Monitoring and Evaluation Programme (EMEP) (2014); UNFCCC (2014), Greenhouse Gas Inventory Data.

StatLink http://dx.doi.org/10.1787/888933261806

Table 1.3. **SO_X emissions and intensities**

	Total SO_X emissions			Intensities per unit of GDP		Intensities per capita		GDP
	1 000 tonnes	% change		Kg/1 000 USD	% change	Kg/cap	% change	% change
	2012 or latest	1990-2012	2000-12	2012 or latest	2000-12	2012 or latest	2000-12	2000-12
Australia	2 334	50	-1	2.7	-31	103	-17	44
Austria	17	-77	-46	0.1	-55	2	-48	21
Belgium	48	-87	-72	0.1	-76	4	-74	18
Canada	1 288	-58	-45	1.0	-57	37	-52	27
Chile	..	..	..	..	..	..	..	68
Czech Republic	158	-92	-40	0.6	-57	15	-42	38
Denmark	12	-93	-60	0.1	-63	2	-62	8
Estonia	41	-85	-58	1.6	-73	31	-57	58
Finland	52	-79	-35	0.3	-46	10	-38	20
France	232	-82	-63	0.1	-68	4	-66	16
Germany	427	-92	-33	0.1	-41	5	-33	14
Greece	245	-49	-51	1.0	-51	22	-51	1
Hungary	32	-96	-92	0.2	-94	3	-92	22
Iceland	84	295	142	7.1	79	262	113	35
Ireland	23	-87	-83	0.1	-87	5	-86	31
Israel	174	..	-39	0.8	-58	22	-50	49
Italy	178	-90	-76	0.1	-77	3	-78	1
Japan	937	-25	-21	0.2	-28	7	-21	9
Korea	434	-47	-12	0.3	-45	9	-16	63
Luxembourg	2	-87	-39	0.1	-55	4	-50	33
Mexico	..	..	..	..	..	..	..	30
Netherlands	34	-82	-53	0.1	-59	2	-55	15
New Zealand	78	34	9	0.7	-19	18	-5	35
Norway	17	-68	-39	0.1	-49	3	-45	21
Poland	853	..	-41	1.2	-62	22	-42	56
Portugal	59	-82	-78	0.3	-78	6	-78	2
Slovak Republic	59	-89	-54	0.5	-72	11	-54	67
Slovenia	10	-95	-89	0.2	-91	5	-89	27
Spain	408	-81	-73	0.3	-78	9	-76	21
Sweden	28	-74	-33	0.1	-47	3	-38	26
Switzerland	11	-73	-32	0.0	-45	1	-38	24
Turkey	2 739	57	17	2.7	-28	36	5	62
United Kingdom	426	-89	-65	0.2	-71	7	-68	21
United States	4 695	-78	-68	0.3	-74	15	-71	22
OECD	**16 053**	**-70**	**-51**	**0.4**	**-59**	**14**	**-54**	**22**
OECD Asia-Oceania	3 981	..	-9	0.6	-25	19	-13	24
OECD Europe	6 195	-75	-43	0.4	-53	11	-47	19

Note: See the Annex for country notes.

Source: OECD (2014) "Air Emissions by Source", *OECD Environment Statistics* (database); European Monitoring and Evaluation Programme (EMEP) (2014); UNFCCC (2014), Greenhouse Gas Inventory Data.

StatLink http://dx.doi.org/10.1787/888933262274

Figure 1.14. **NO_X emission intensities per capita, 2000, 2012**

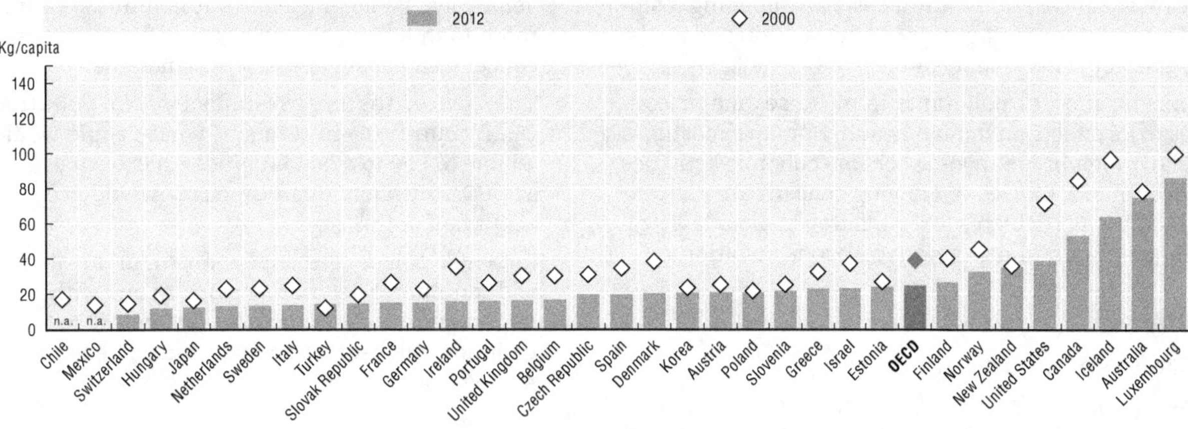

Source: OECD (2014) "Air Emissions by Source", *OECD Environment Statistics* (database); European Monitoring and Evaluation Programme (EMEP) (2014); UNFCCC (2014), Greenhouse Gas Inventory Data.

StatLink http://dx.doi.org/10.1787/888933261818

Table 1.4. **NO_X emissions and intensities**

	Total NO_X emissions			Intensities per unit of GDP		Intensities per capita		GDP
	1 000 tonnes	% change		kg/1 000 USD	% change	kg/cap	% change	% change
	2012 or latest	1990-2012	2000-12	2012 or latest	2000-12	2012 or latest	2000-12	2000-12
Australia	1 707	33	14	2.0	-21	75	-5	44
Austria	178	-8	-13	0.6	-28	21	-17	21
Belgium	190	-49	-39	0.5	-49	17	-44	18
Canada	1 862	-27	-28	1.4	-44	53	-37	27
Chile	..	..	..	..	..	..	..	68
Czech Republic	211	-72	-34	0.8	-53	20	-36	38
Denmark	115	-58	-44	0.6	-48	21	-47	8
Estonia	32	-56	-14	1.3	-46	24	-11	58
Finland	146	-51	-31	0.8	-42	27	-34	20
France	982	-47	-38	0.5	-46	15	-42	16
Germany	1 269	-56	-34	0.4	-42	15	-34	14
Greece	259	-21	-28	1.1	-29	23	-29	1
Hungary	122	-51	-39	0.7	-50	12	-37	22
Iceland	21	-25	-25	1.7	-44	64	-34	35
Ireland	74	-40	-46	0.4	-58	16	-55	31
Israel	182	..	-23	0.8	-47	23	-38	49
Italy	849	-58	-41	0.5	-41	14	-45	1
Japan	1 627	-20	-23	0.4	-30	13	-24	9
Korea	1 040	19	-7	0.7	-42	21	-13	63
Luxembourg	45	17	4	1.3	-22	86	-13	33
Mexico	..	..	..	..	..	..	..	30
Netherlands	227	-59	-39	0.3	-47	14	-42	15
New Zealand	158	60	13	1.3	-17	36	-2	35
Norway	166	-13	-19	0.7	-33	33	-28	21
Poland	817	-31	-3	1.2	-38	21	-4	56
Portugal	170	-31	-38	0.7	-39	16	-39	2
Slovak Republic	81	-62	-25	0.7	-55	15	-25	67
Slovenia	45	-26	-11	0.9	-30	22	-14	27
Spain	928	-31	-34	0.7	-46	20	-43	21
Sweden	132	-51	-37	0.4	-50	14	-41	26
Switzerland	69	-51	-36	0.2	-48	9	-42	24
Turkey	1 088	93	29	1.1	-21	14	16	62
United Kingdom	1 057	-63	-41	0.5	-52	17	-46	21
United States	12 258	-46	-40	0.9	-51	39	-46	22
OECD	**28 108**	**-40**	**-32**	**0.7**	**-44**	**25**	**-37**	22
OECD Asia-Oceania	4 728	..	-8	0.7	-24	22	-12	24
OECD Europe	9 273	-46	-30	0.6	-41	17	-34	19

Note: See the Annex for country notes.

Source: OECD (2014) "Air Emissions by Source", *OECD Environment Statistics* (database); European Monitoring and Evaluation Programme (EMEP) (2014); UNFCCC (2014), Greenhouse Gas Inventory Data.

StatLink http://dx.doi.org/10.1787/888933262287

Particulate emissions and population exposure

Degraded air quality can have substantial economic and social consequences, from health costs and building restoration needs to reduced agricultural output, forest damage and a generally lower quality of life.

The concentration of pollutants in air raises major concerns as to its effects on human health. Human exposure is particularly high in urban areas where economic activities are concentrated. Causes of growing concern are concentrations of fine particulates ($PM_{2.5}$), nitrogen dioxide (NO_2), toxic air pollutants, and ground-level ozone pollution.

Definitions

The indicators presented here refer to:

- Emissions of fine particulates from human activities, given as quantities of $PM_{2.5}$. The data show emission intensities per capita and changes over time.
- Population exposure to air pollution by fine particulates. The indicators reflect the estimated annual mean exposure level of an average resident to outdoor particulate matter, expressed as population weighted $PM_{2.5}$ levels; and the share of population exposed to levels exceeding 10 micrograms per m^3 (WHO long-term guideline value). They provide a general indication of the relative risk of PM pollution.

Fine particulates ($PM_{2.5}$) refer to suspended particulates smaller than 2.5 microns in diameter that are capable of penetrating very deep into the respiratory tract and causing severe health effects. They are potentially more toxic than small particulates (PM_{10}) and may include heavy metals and toxic organic substances.

The indicators shown here provide only a partial view of air pollution. They should be complemented with information on other air pollutants, and be read in connection with data on socio-demographic patterns, climatic conditions, and emission and fuel standards.

Overview

Over the past two decades, urban air quality has continued to improve slowly with respect to sulphur dioxide (SO_2) concentrations, and human exposure to small particulates (PM_{10}) has been decreasing.

But acute ground-level ozone pollution episodes in both urban and rural areas, NO_2 concentrations, fine particulates ($PM_{2.5}$), and toxic air pollutants are of growing concern. This is largely due to the concentration of pollution sources in urban areas and to the increasing use of private vehicles for urban trips.

Some groups of the population are especially vulnerable to air pollution. The very young and the very old are more at risk than the remainder of the population.

In several OECD countries per capita emissions of fine particulates and the share of the population exposed to $PM_{2.5}$ concentrations above the WHO guideline value have fallen. But, in about half of the countries, more than 90% of the population is still exposed to concentrations above the WHO guideline.

The cost of the health impact of air pollution in OECD countries – in terms of what people would be willing to pay to avoid fatalities – has been estimated at USD 1.7 trillion. Road transport would account for about half of this cost.

If no new policies are implemented, urban air quality will continue to deteriorate globally, and with increasing urbanisation and population ageing, outdoor air pollution will become the top cause of environment-related deaths by 2050.

Comparability

International data on particulate emissions are available for many but not all OECD countries. The estimation methods for emissions, the extent of sources and particles included in estimation, may differ from one country to another.

International data on exposure to air pollution exist, but often are scattered (sources: WHO, World Bank, OECD, EEA). The most comprehensive effort to measure exposure levels worldwide is the Global Burden of Diseases, Injuries, and Risk Factors Study (GBD).

Sources

OECD (2014), "Air Emissions by Source", *OECD Environment Statistics* (database), *http://dx.doi.org/10.1787/data-00598-en.*

European Monitoring and Evaluation Programme (EMEP) (2014), *www.emep.int.*

World Bank (2015), *World Development Indicators, http://data.worldbank.org/data-catalog/world-developmentindicators.*

Further information

OECD (2015a), *How's Life? 2015: Measuring Well-Being*, OECD Publishing, Paris, *http://dx.doi.org/10.1787/how_life-2015-en.*

OECD (2015b), *OECD Regions at a Glance 2015*, OECD Publishing, Paris, forthcoming.

OECD (2014a), *How's Life in Your Region?: Measuring Regional and LocalWell-Being for Policy Making*, OECD Publishing, *http://dx.doi.org/10.1787/9789264217416-en.*

OECD (2014b), *The Cost of Air Pollution: Health Impacts of Road Transport*, OECD Publishing, Paris, *http://dx.doi.org/10.1787/9789264210448-en.*

OECD (2012), *OECD Environmental Outlook to 2050: The Consequences of Inaction*, OECD Publishing, Paris, *http://dx.doi.org/10.1787/9789264122246-en.*

UNECE (2014), "Convention on Long-Range Transboundary Air Pollution", *www.unece.org/env/lrtap/multi_h1.html.*

Information on data for Israel: *http://dx.doi.org/10.1787/888932315602.*

Figure 1.15. **Emission intensities of fine particulates ($PM_{2.5}$)**

Emissions per capita, selected countries, 2012, 2000

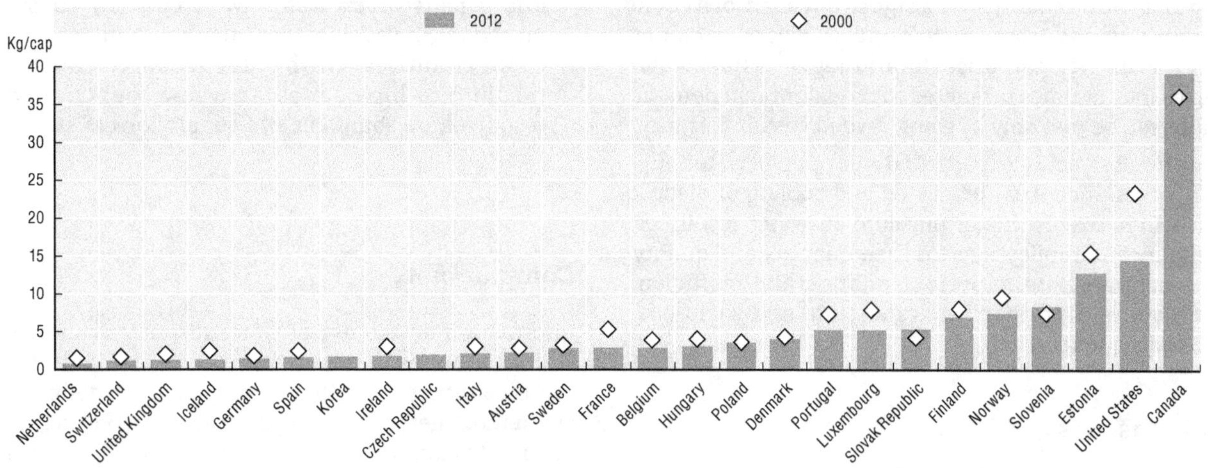

1. See the Annex for country notes.
Source: OECD (2014), "Air Emissions by Source", *OECD Environment Statistics* (database); European Monitoring and Evaluation Programme (EMEP) (2014).

StatLink http://dx.doi.org/10.1787/888933261822

Figure 1.16. **Population exposure to fine particulates ($PM_{2.5}$)**

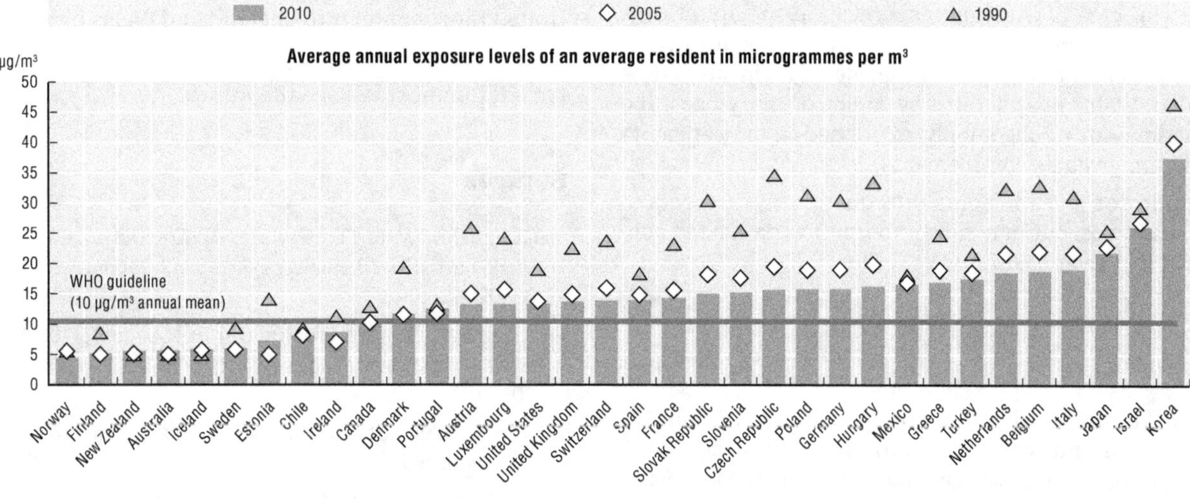

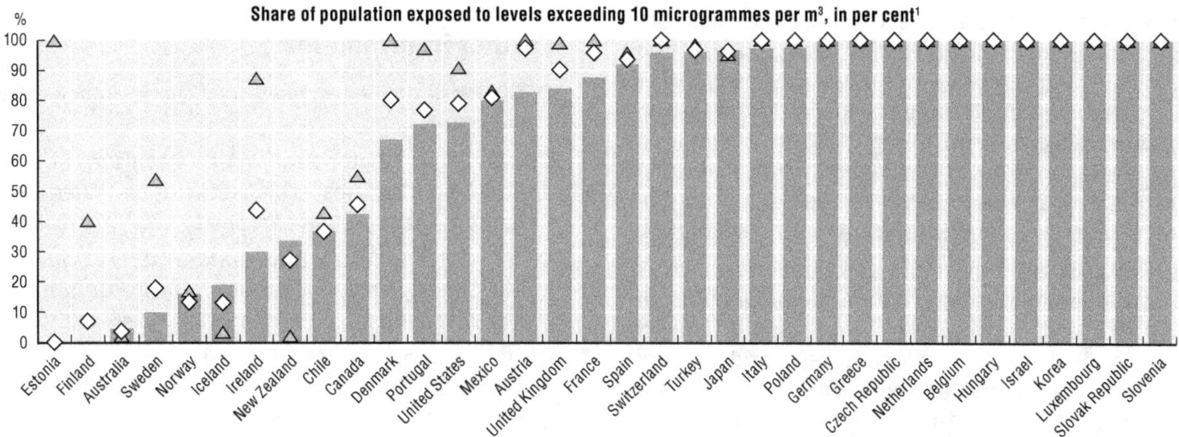

1. WHO guideline value
2. See the Annex for country notes.
Source: World Bank (2015), *World Development Indicators* (database).

StatLink http://dx.doi.org/10.1787/888933261830

Use of freshwater resources

Freshwater resources are of major environmental, economic and social importance. Their distribution varies widely among and within countries. If a significant share of a country's water comes from transboundary rivers, tensions between countries can arise. In arid regions, freshwater resources may at times be limited to the extent that demand for water can be met only by going beyond sustainable use.

Freshwater abstractions, particularly for public water supply, irrigation, industrial processes and cooling of electric power plants, exert a major pressure on water resources, with significant implications for their quantity and quality. Main concerns relate to overexploitation and inefficient use of water and to their environmental and socio-economic consequences.

Definitions

The indicator presented here refers to the intensity of use of freshwater resources (or water stress). It is expressed as gross abstractions of freshwater taken from ground or surface waters in % of total available renewable freshwater resources (including water inflows from neighbouring countries), in % of internal resources (i.e. precipitation – evapotranspiration), and per capita. Water used for hydroelectricity generation (which is considered an in situ use) is excluded. Water abstractions by major primary uses and abstractions for public supply, expressed in m^3 per capita per day, are given as complements.

This indicator gives insights into quantitative aspects of water resources, but may hide important variations at subnational (e.g. river basin) level.

Overview

Over the last century, the estimated growth in global water demand was more than double the rate of population growth, with agriculture being the largest user of water.

In the 1980s, some countries stabilised their abstractions through more efficient irrigation techniques, the decline of water-intensive industries, increased use of more efficient technologies and reduced losses in pipe networks. Since the mid-1990s, OECD-wide trends in water abstractions have been generally stable. In some countries this is due to increased use of alternative water sources, including water reuse and desalination.

The use of irrigation water in the OECD area slightly declined compared to agricultural production, but in about half of the countries it increased driven by expansion in the irrigated area. In semi-arid areas in North America and the Mediterranean region, groundwater sustains an increasing share of irrigation.

Water stress levels vary greatly among and within countries. Most face seasonal or local water quantity problems, and several have extensive arid or semi-arid regions where water availability is a constraint on economic development. In more than one-third of OECD countries, freshwater resources are under medium to high stress. In a few countries water resources are abundant and population density is low.

Comparability

Information on the use of water resources can be derived from water resource account. It is available for most OECD countries, but often incomplete. The definitions and estimation methods employed may vary considerably from country to country and over time. In general, data availability and quality are best for water abstractions for public supply. For some countries the data refer to water permits and not to actual abstractions.

OECD totals are estimates based on linear interpolations to fill missing values, and exclude Chile. Data for the United Kingdom refer to England and Wales only.

Latest year available: data prior to 2009 were not considered.

For additional notes, see the Annex.

Sources

OECD (2015), "Water: Freshwater Abstractions", *OECD Environment Statistics* (database), *http://dx.doi.org/10.1787/data-00602-en.*

OECD (2014), "Water: Freshwater Resources", *OECD Environment Statistics* (database), *http://dx.doi.org/10.1787/data-00603-en.*

FAO (2015), *AquaStat* (database), *www.fao.org/nr/water/aquastat/main/index.stm.*

FAO (2015), FAOSTAT (database), *http://faostat3.fao.org.*

Further information

OECD Work on Water, *www.oecd.org/environment/resources/water.htm.*

OECD (2015), "Water Resources Allocation: Sharing Risks and Opportunities", *OECD Studies on Water*, OECD Publishing, Paris, *http://dx.doi.org/10.1787/9789264229631-en.*

OECD (2012), *OECD Environmental Outlook to 2050: The Consequences of Inaction*, OECD Publishing, Paris, *http://dx.doi.org/10.1787/9789264122246-en0.*

United Nations WWAP (World Water Assessment Programme) (2015), *The United Nations World Water Development Report 2015: Water for a Sustainable World*, Paris, UNESCO.

Information on data for Israel: *http://dx.doi.org/10.1787/888932315602.*

Figure 1.17. **Gross freshwater abstractions per capita**

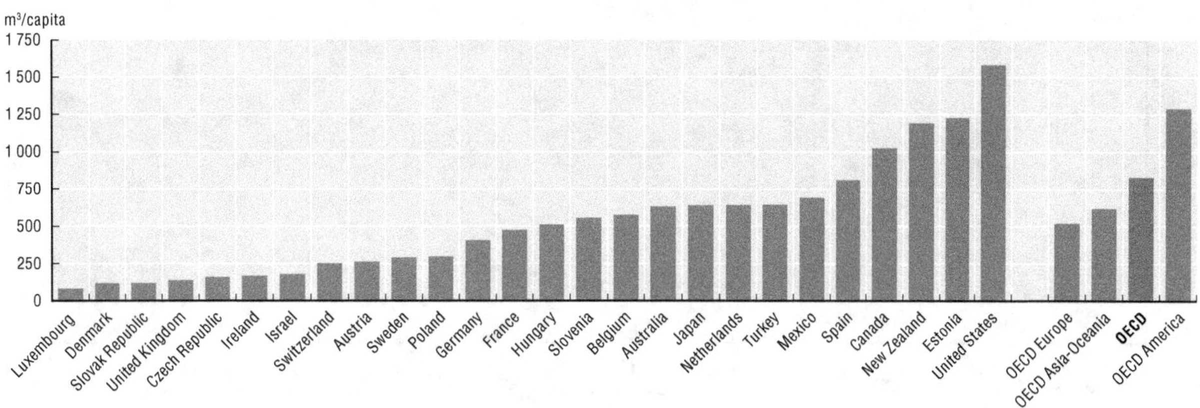

Source: OECD (2015), "Water: Freshwater Abstractions", *OECD Environment Statistics* (database).

StatLink http://dx.doi.org/10.1787/888933261841

Table 1.5. **Freshwater resources and abstractions**

	Intensity of use of freshwater resources							Irrigation		
	Abstractions as % of available resources			Abstractions per capita			Abstractions per area of irrigated land	Irrigated area as % of arable land		
	%	Absolute change		m³/capita/year	% change		m³/ha/year	%	% change	
	2013 or latest	Since 1990	Since 2000	2013 or latest	Since 1990	Since 2000	2013 or latest	2012	1990-2012	2000-12
Australia	3.6	..	-2.1	630	..	-45	2 480	5	41	7
Austria	2.9	..	..	260	..	..	150	8	77	27
Belgium	31.0	..	-6.8	570	..	-22	..	3	-25	-25
Canada	1.0	-0.3	..	1 030	-36	..	1 730	2	24	14
Chile	..	..	..	..	..	..	..	62	64	19
Czech Republic	10.3	..	-1.7	160	..	-16	780	1	12	-6
Denmark	4.0	-3.7	-0.5	120	-52	-14	220	18	8	-8
Estonia	13.2	-12.8	1.3	1 230	-40	15	0	1	20	36
Finland	..	..	..	..	..	..	0	3	9	-24
France	15.7	-4.0	-1.4	470	-29	-15	1 120	13	30	0
Germany	17.2	-6.9	-2.6	400	-30	-12	280	5	39	34
Greece	..	..	..	..	..	..	5 060	42	48	23
Hungary	4.3	-1.1	-1.3	510	-16	-21	1 270	4	-3	-24
Iceland	..	..	..	..	..	..	..	..	..	..
Ireland	1.5	..	..	170	..	..	..	..	..	..
Israel	50.2	-16.5	-14.5	180	-54	-36	..	58	22	20
Italy	..	..	..	..	..	..	..	41	28	21
Japan	19.7	-1.8	-1.3	640	-11	-7	21 540	54	0	-1
Korea	..	..	..	..	..	..	..	45	-4	-2
Luxembourg	2.6	..	-1.1	80	..	-43	..	..	..	..
Mexico	17.3	..	2.4	690	..	-1	9 450	25	7	1
Netherlands	11.7	3.0	2.0	640	21	15	47	46	-3	-12
New Zealand	1.1	..	0.4	1 190	..	45	4 120	111	965	503
Norway	..	..	..	..	..	..	..	11	-2	-27
Poland	17.8	-6.2	-1.2	300	-26	-6	820	1	-58	38
Portugal	..	..	..	..	..	..	6 960	30	7	-9
Slovak Republic	0.8	-1.8	-0.7	120	-71	-46	240	6	-59	-47
Slovenia	3.6	..	..	550	..	..	330	3	256	105
Spain	33.6	0.4	0.7	810	-15	-11	6 150	22	33	10
Sweden	1.4	-0.1	0.0	290	-17	-5	380	6	57	24
Switzerland	3.8	-1.3	-1.1	250	-37	-30	2 220	15	151	68
Turkey	20.0	..	..	640	..	..	7 790	22	49	22
United Kingdom	11.0	-6.0	-5.0	137	-42	-36	1 240	2	-35	-63
United States	19.8	1.1	0.3	1 580	-15	-7	6 010	17	17	10
OECD	**9.9**	**0.3**	**0.0**	**829**	**-13**	**-8**	**6 821**	**15**	**19**	**9**
OECD America	9.4	0.4	0.2	1 291	-19	-10	6 990	15	15	8
OECD Asia-Oceania	9.6	0.1	-0.8	616	-9	-12	11 516	12	17	8
OECD Europe	11.5	-0.1	0.1	518	-11	-5	4 966	16	28	10

Note: See the Annex for country notes.

Source: FAO (2015), FAOSTAT database; OECD (2015), "Water: Freshwater Abstractions", "Water: Freshwater Resources", *OECD Environment Statistics* (database).

StatLink http://dx.doi.org/10.1787/888933262294

Figure 1.18. **Total renewable freshwater resources per capita, long-term annual average values**

1 000 m³/capita
120
100
80
60
40
20
0
528
Israel
Korea
Czech Republic
Poland
Belgium
Italy
Germany
Spain
United Kingdom
Denmark
France
Luxembourg
Turkey
Japan
Mexico
Netherlands
Greece
Switzerland
Portugal
United States
Estonia
Austria
Ireland
Hungary
Slovak Republic
Slovenia
Australia
Sweden
Finland
Chile
Norway
Canada
New Zealand
Iceland

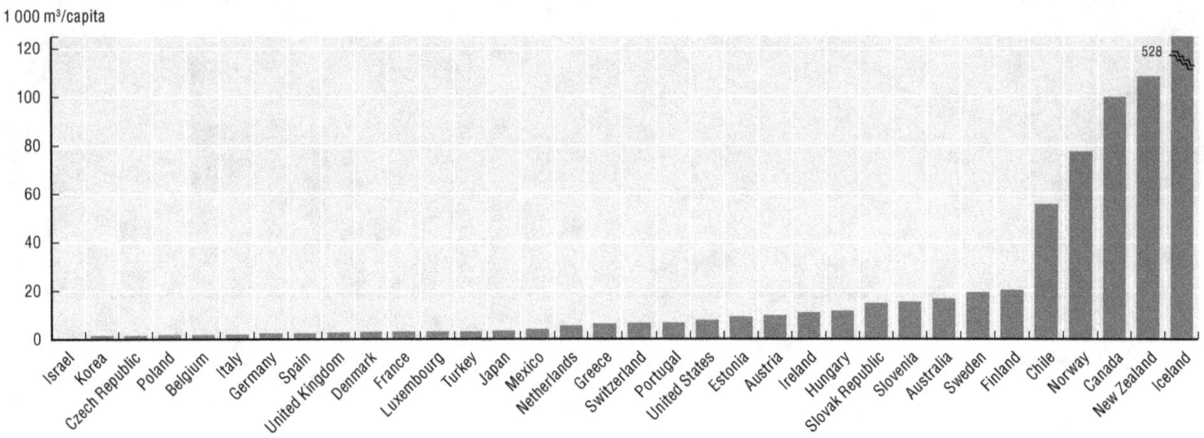

Source: OECD (2015), "Water: Freshwater Resources", *OECD Environment Statistics* (database).

StatLink http://dx.doi.org/10.1787/888933261851

Figure 1.19. **Intensity of use of freshwater resources, 2013 or latest available year**

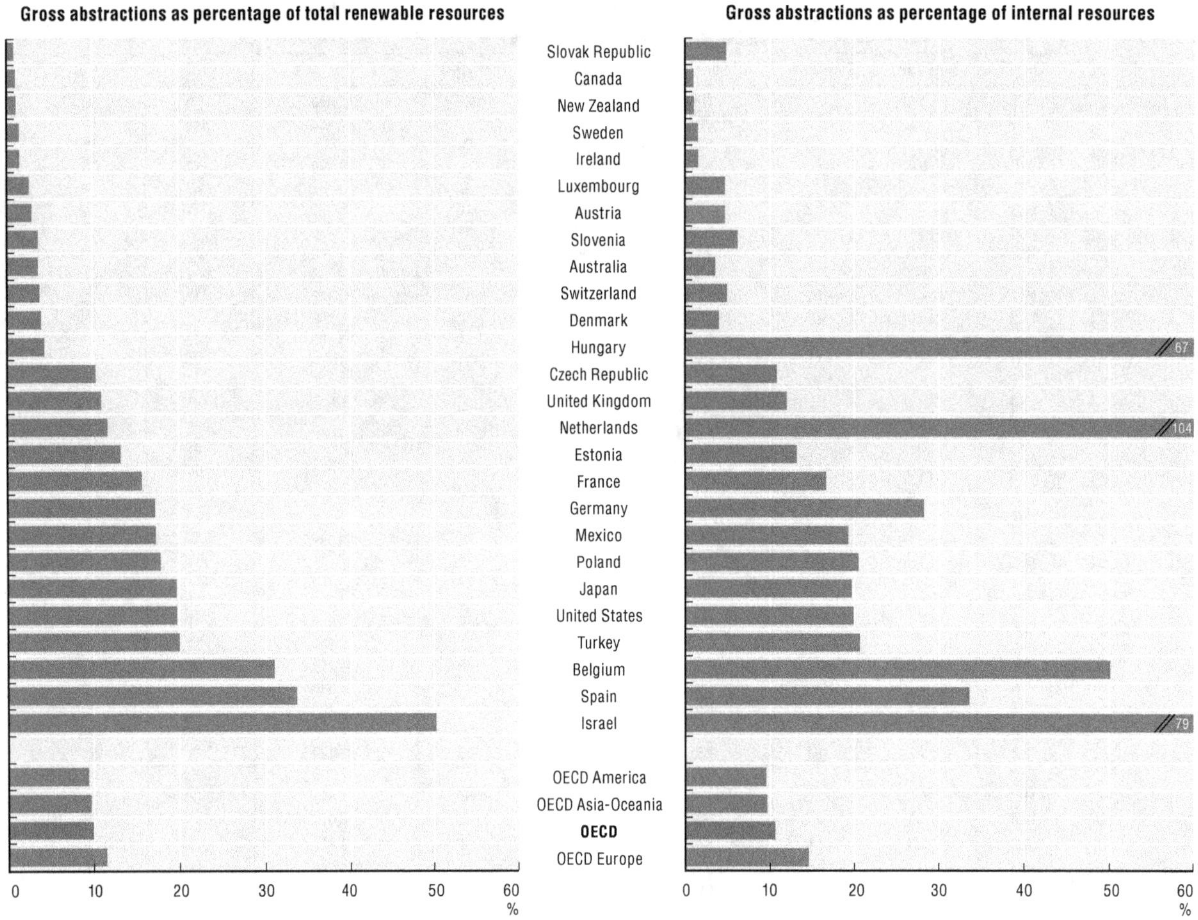

Gross abstractions as percentage of total renewable resources
Gross abstractions as percentage of internal resources
Slovak Republic
Canada
New Zealand
Sweden
Ireland
Luxembourg
Austria
Slovenia
Australia
Switzerland
Denmark
Hungary
Czech Republic
United Kingdom
Netherlands
Estonia
France
Germany
Mexico
Poland
Japan
United States
Turkey
Belgium
Spain
Israel
OECD America
OECD Asia-Oceania
OECD
OECD Europe
67
104
79
0
10
20
30
40
50
60
%

* Water stress: < 10%: low; 10-20%: medium-high; > 40%: high.
Source: OECD (2015), "Water: Freshwater Abstractions", *OECD Environment Statistics* (database); OECD (2015), "Water: Freshwater Resources", *OECD Environment Statistics* (database).

StatLink http://dx.doi.org/10.1787/888933261866

Figure 1.20. **Freshwater abstractions by major primary uses**

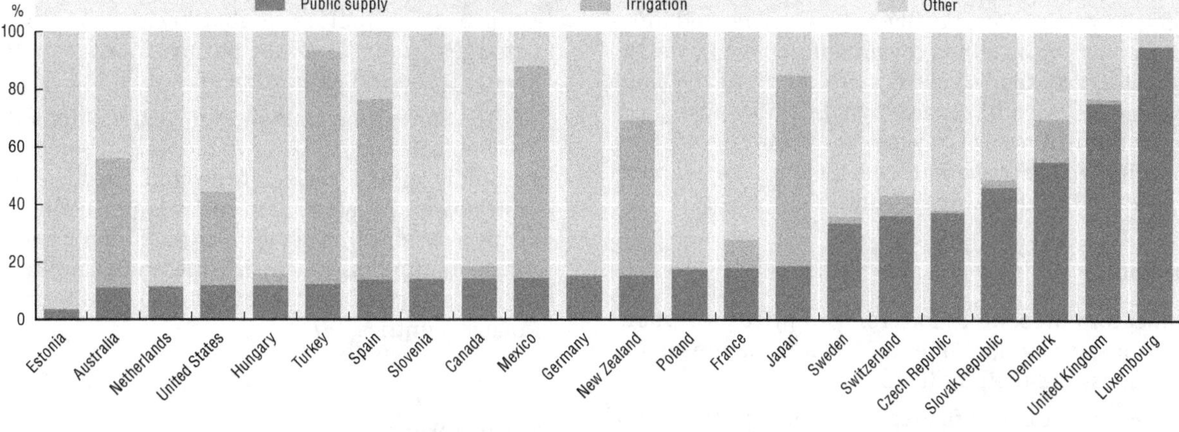

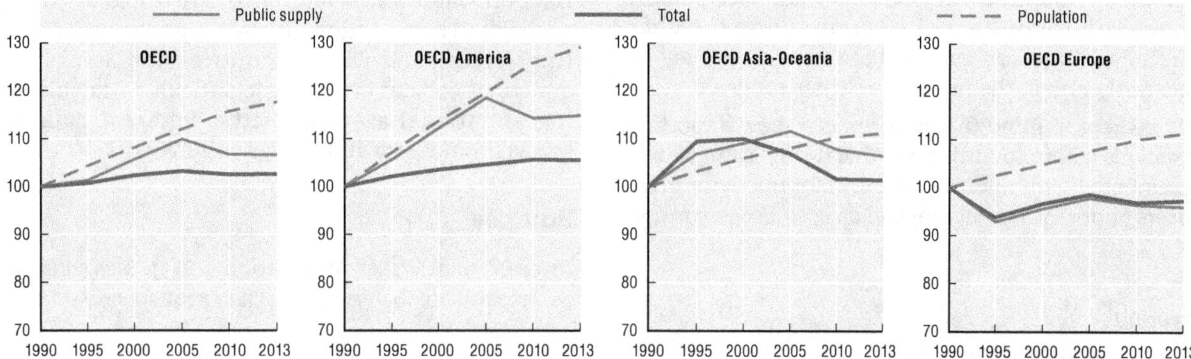

Source: OECD (2015), "Water: Freshwater Abstractions", *OECD Environment Statistics* (database); OECD (2015), *OECD Historical Population Data and Projections Statistics* (database).

StatLink http://dx.doi.org/10.1787/888933261871

Figure 1.21. **Abstractions for public supply per capita, 2013 or latest available year**

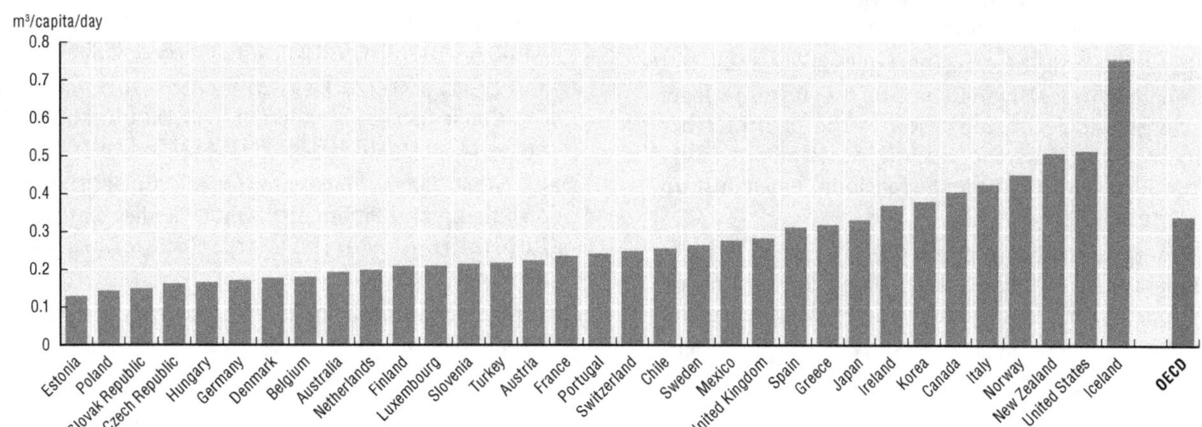

Source: OECD (2015), "Water: Freshwater Abstractions", *OECD Environment Statistics* (database).

StatLink http://dx.doi.org/10.1787/888933261884

Water pricing for public supply

Pricing of water and water-related services is an important mechanism for managing demand and promoting efficient use of water, for allocating water among competing uses and for generating finance to invest in water-related infrastructure and services. When consumers do not pay the full cost of water, they tend to use it inefficiently. At the same time, when the price levels are high, this may pose problems of continued access to water for poorer consumers, and the affordability of the water bill for low income households needs to be taken into account.

Definitions

The indicators presented here refer to prices for public water supply to households and small businesses in selected cities, and their tariff structure.

The prices refer to 2013 figures, expressed in USD as of 31 December 2013. The data are expressed in US dollars per cubic metre supplied. They refer to the prices paid by customers and to an annual consumption of 200 m^3 per year, to facilitate comparison between cities. They do not necessarily reflect the full cost of water services.

It should be kept in mind that water prices show important local variations within countries, and that the indicator should be supplemented with information on water prices for other major users (industry, agriculture) and on cost recovery ratios.

Overview

Today OECD countries are covering more of the costs associated with the provision of water services. This is reflected in the level of prices, which have increased, at times substantially, over the last decade, and in the structure of tariffs, which better reflect consumption and treatment costs.

Tariff structures for water supply vary across and within countries. Diversity within a country reflects the degree of decentralisation of the tariff-setting process, as well as the varying costs of providing water services in different locations, especially in rural areas.

An emerging trend in some OECD countries is the increasing use of fixed charges alongside volumetric components, or the progressive increase in the weight of fixed charges in the overall bill. Water pricing is also increasingly complemented by a range of other approaches, including abstraction and pollution charges, tradable water permits, smart metering, water reuse and innovation.

At the same time, demand for higher standards and technologies for drinking water purification and sanitation is rising because of the continued presence of nitrates and pesticides in many water bodies, along with new concerns about micro-pollutants and endocrine disruptors. Addressing these challenges will be costly, and could lead to an increase in water prices in many countries.

Comparability

Data on water prices and tariff structures are only partly available. The variations in water prices and price structures across and within countries and across different groups of consumers make it difficult to calculate meaningful national averages. Little coherent data exist on prices for industry and for agriculture.

Sources

International Water Association (2014), *International Statistics for Water Services*, *www.iwa-network.org*.

Further information

OECD Work on Water, *www.oecd.org/environment/resources/water.htm*.

OECD (2015), "Water Resources Allocation: Sharing Risks and Opportunities", *OECD Studies on Water*, OECD Publishing, Paris, *http://dx.doi.org/10.1787/9789264229631-en*.

OECD (2012), *OECD Environmental Outlook to 2050: The Consequences of Inaction*, OECD Publishing, Paris, *http://dx.doi.org/10.1787/9789264122246-en*.

OECD (2009), "Managing Water for All: An OECD Perspective on Pricing and Financing", *OECD Studies on Water*, OECD Publishing, Paris, *http://dx.doi.org/10.1787/9789264059498-en*.

Information on data for Israel: *http://dx.doi.org/10.1787/888932315602*.

Figure 1.22. **Water prices in selected major cities, 2013**

Total annual charges and tariff structure

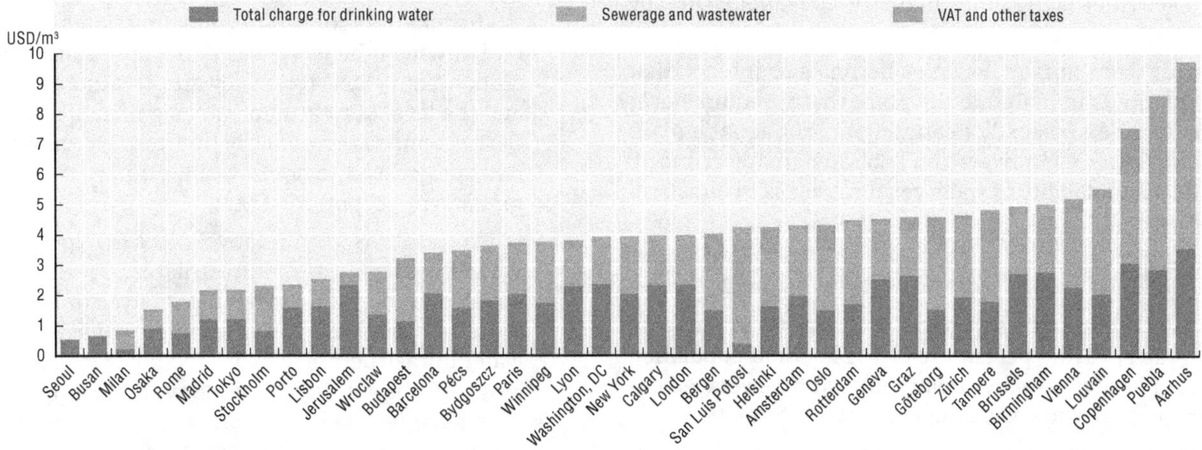

Source: International Water Association (2014), *International Statistics for Water Services.*

StatLink http://dx.doi.org/10.1787/888933261897

Table 1.6. **Water prices in selected major cities, 2013**

Total annual charges

	City	USD/m³		City	USD/m³		City	USD/m³
Austria	Graz	4.59	Hungary	Budapest	3.21	Norway	Bergen	4.03
	Innsbruck	5.00		Debrecen	2.43		Oslo	4.32
	Linz	3.18		Miskolc	2.59		Trondheim	5.00
	Salzburg	6.15		Pécs	3.48	Poland	Bydgoszcz	3.64
	Vienna	5.20		Kaposvár	2.05		Wroclaw	2.77
Belgium	Louvain	5.52	Israel	Jerusalem	2.76		Radom	2.75
	Antwerp	4.29	Italy	Bologna	2.40		Tarnow	2.86
	Brussels	4.95		Milan	0.83	Portugal	Lisbon	2.57
	Liège	6.24		Naples	1.78		Porto	2.39
	Kortrijk	5.62		Rome	1.78		Braga	2.38
	Genk	5.11		Turin	2.25		Coimbra	2.69
	Charleroi	5.95	Korea	Seoul	0.53		Faro	2.32
Canada	Calgary	3.98		Busan	0.65	Spain	Barcelona	3.40
	Winnipeg	3.76		Daegu	0.55		Bilbao	2.16
	Regina	4.52		Incheon	0.61		Madrid	2.17
	Richmond	5.04		Gwangju	0.50		Sevilla	2.99
	Durham	3.27		Daejeon	0.49		Valencia	2.69
Denmark	Aalborg	9.48		Ulsan	0.83	Sweden	Stockholm	2.52
	Aarhus	9.80		Gyeounggi	0.59		Göteborg	4.59
	Copenhagen	7.63	Japan	Nagoya	1.67		Malmö	3.22
	Esbjerg	8.52		Osaka	1.53		Uppsala	4.55
	Odense	9.37		Hiroshima	1.90		Linköping	4.64
Finland	Espoo	4.63		Fukuoka	2.24	Switzerland	Geneva	4.52
	Helsinki	4.63		Sapporo	2.27		Zürich	4.65
	Oulu	5.21		Sendai	2.79		Lausanne	4.36
	Tampere	5.30		Tokyo	2.18		Basel	4.57
	Turku	6.39		Yokohama	2.02		Bern	6.22
	Vantaa	4.63	Mexico	San Luis Potosi	4.25	England and Wales	Birmingham	5.02
France	Bordeaux	4.43		Guadalajara	0.87		Cardiff	5.85
	Lille	5.03		León, Guanajuato	4.87		London	3.98
	Lyon	4.04		Monterrey	4.72		Manchester	5.77
	Paris	4.16		Puebla	8.62		Leeds	5.18
	Strasbourg	4.19	Netherlands	Amsterdam	4.53	United States	New York	3.94
	Reims	4.32		Rotterdam	4.71		Washington, DC	4.18
	Nancy	4.15		Den Haag	5.00		Los Angeles	2.72
	Le Havre	5.83		Utrecht	4.28		Chicago	1.46
	Marseille	4.75		Eindhoven	3.35		Denver	2.64
	Brest	6.15		Maastricht	4.16		Miami	1.01

Source: International Water Association (2014), *International Statistics for Water Services.*

StatLink http://dx.doi.org/10.1787/888933262305

Wastewater treatment

Water quality (physical, chemical, microbial, biological) is affected by water abstraction, by pollution loads from human activities (agriculture, industry, households) and by climate and weather.

If pressure from human activities becomes so intense that water quality is impaired to the point that it requires ever more advanced and costly treatment, or that aquatic plant and animal species in rivers and lakes are greatly reduced, then the sustainability of water resource use is in question.

Definitions

The indicator presented here refers to sewage treatment connection rates, i.e. the percentage of the national population connected to a wastewater treatment plant. Sewerage connection rates are shown as complementary information.

"Connected" means actually connected to a wastewater treatment plant through a public sewage network. It does not take into account independent private facilities (e.g. septic tanks), used where public systems are not economic.

The data show total connection rates and the extent of secondary and/or tertiary sewage treatment to provide an indication of efforts to reduce pollution loads.

- Primary treatment: physical and/or chemical process involving settlement of suspended solids, or other process in which the BOD5 of the incoming wastewater is reduced by at least 20% before discharge and the total suspended solids are reduced by at least 50%.
- Secondary treatment: process generally involving biological treatment with a secondary settlement or other process, with a BOD removal of at least 70% and a COD removal of at least 75%.
- Tertiary treatment: treatment of nitrogen and/or phosphorous and/or any other pollutant affecting the quality or a specific use of water (microbiological pollution, colour, etc.).

This indicator should be read in connection with information on public wastewater treatment expenditure. It should be related to an optimal national connection rate, recognising that the optimal connection rate is not necessarily 100%: it may vary among countries and depends on geographical features and on the spatial distribution of habitats.

Overview

In recent decades, OECD countries have been progressing with basic domestic water pollution abatement and with sewerage and wastewater treatment infrastructure.

- The share of the population connected to a municipal wastewater treatment plant rose from about 50% in the early 1980s to over 60% in the early 1990s and is close to 80% today.
- Due to varying settlement patterns, economic and environmental conditions, starting dates and the rate at which the work was done, the share of population connected to wastewater treatment plants and the level of treatment vary significantly among OECD countries: secondary and tertiary treatment have progressed in some while primary treatment remains important in others.
- OECD countries with relatively low GDP per capita are still in the phase of infrastructure development, which can command investment of the order of 1% of GDP. Those OECD countries that established their water infrastructure decades ago now face the challenge of upgrading ageing networks. Some countries have reached the economic limit in terms of sewerage connection; they must find other ways of serving small or isolated settlements and ensuring proper control and functioning of small independent treatment facilities.

Comparability

Data on the share of the population connected to wastewater treatment plants are available for almost all OECD countries. In some countries, data relate to population equivalents and are thus not fully comparable. Information on the level of treatment and on treatment charges remains partial.

Data include estimates.

For additional notes, see the Annex.

Sources

OECD (2015), "Wastewater Treatment (% Population Connected)", *OECD Environment Statistics* (database), *http://dx.doi.org/10.1787/data-00604-en*.

Further information

OECD Work on Water, *www.oecd.org/environment/resources/water.htm*.

OECD (2012), *OECD Environmental Outlook to 2050: The Consequences of Inaction*, OECD Publishing, Paris, *http://dx.doi.org/10.1787/9789264122246-en*.

Information on data for Israel: *http://dx.doi.org/10.1787/888932315602*.

Figure 1.23. **Sewage treatment connection rates, 2013 or latest available year**

% of national population connected to a wastewater treatment plant

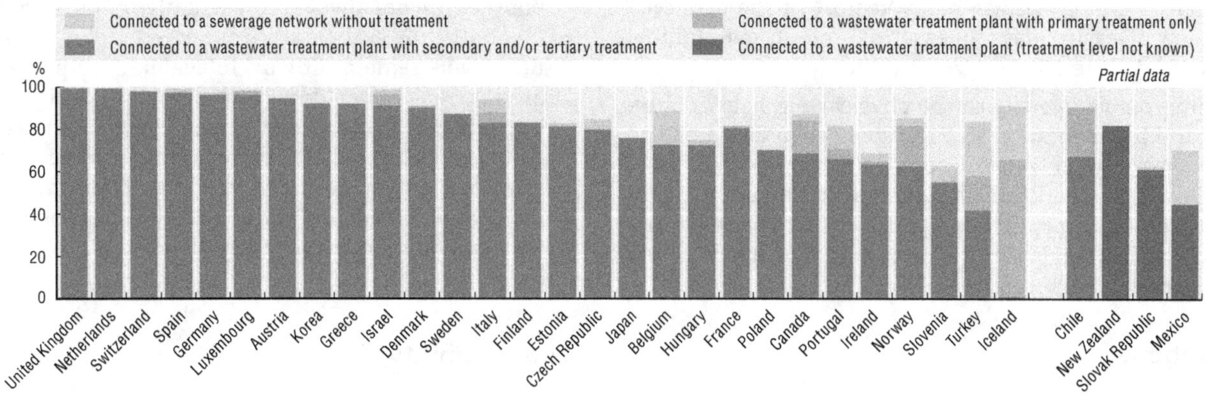

Source: OECD (2015), "Wastewater Treatment (% Population Connected)", *OECD Environment Statistics* (database).

StatLink http://dx.doi.org/10.1787/888933261900

Table 1.7. **Sewage treatment connection rates, % of population**

	Sewage treatment connection rates									Sewerage network connection rates
	Early 1990s			Early 2000s			2013 or latest			2013 or latest
	Total	*Of which:* Secondary treatment	*Of which:* Tertiary treatment	Total	*Of which:* Secondary treatment	*Of which:* Tertiary treatment	Total	*Of which:* Secondary treatment	*Of which:* Tertiary treatment	Total
Australia	..	..	..	..	..	..	..	..	..	..
Austria	72	60	7	85	..	..	95	1	94	95
Belgium	..	..	..	41	6	36	73	9	63	88
Canada	62	21	27	87	48	19	84	53	15	87
Chile[Note:]	..	..	..	72	2	48	91	4	63	..
Czech Republic	50	..	..	64	..	..	80	8	72	85
Denmark	85	42	29	88	4	83	91	2	88	91
Estonia	68	31	..	69	28	40	82	7	74	83
Finland[Note:]	76	0	76	80	0	80	83	0	83	83
France	69	..	..	79	51	26	82	44	29	82
Germany	86	32	48	93	5	88	96	3	93	97
Greece	11	11	0	..	..	..	92	6	86	92
Hungary	20	14	1	46	24	6	73	16	57	75
Iceland	2	0	0	33	0	0	66	0	1	91
Ireland	44	21	0	70	21	8	65	49	14	69
Israel	77	32	28	87	40	34	97	39	52	99
Italy	61	..	..	82	..	..	88	34	49	94
Japan	44	42	2	62	54	8	76	55	20	76
Korea	33	..	..	71	69	1	92	10	82	92
Luxembourg	90	..	..	95	66	22	98	27	70	98
Mexico	22	19	0	23	..	..	50	..	..	..
Netherlands	94	84	8	98	17	82	99	1	99	99
New Zealand	80	33	40	81	26	40	82	..	..	..
Norway	57	1	43	74	1	51	82	1	61	85
Poland	34	..	..	54	30	20	70	14	56	70
Portugal	21	11	0	57	26	9	71	47	19	81
Slovak Republic	43	..	..	51	..	..	61	..	..	62
Slovenia	..	..	..	36	15	2	55	33	22	63
Spain	48	..	..	81	65	15	98	29	68	99
Sweden	94	9	85	86	5	81	87	4	83	87
Switzerland	90	28	62	96	22	74	98	11	87	98
Turkey	7	1	0	26	15	4	58	20	22	84
United Kingdom	87	65	14	..	..	..	100	50	50	100
United States	70	34	28	75	34	39	..	..	..	..
OECD	**57**	**34**	**18**	**67**	**34**	**29**	**77**	**28**	**42**	**81**
OECD America	61	29	21	63	29	28	67	28	28	72
OECD Asia-Oceania	42	41	2	65	57	7	81	43	39	81
OECD Europe	59	35	21	71	29	37	84	23	56	89

Note: See the Annex for country notes.

Source: OECD (2015), "Wastewater Treatment (% Population Connected)", *OECD Environment Statistics* (database).

StatLink http://dx.doi.org/10.1787/888933262316

Biological diversity

Biological resources are essential elements of ecosystems and of natural capital; they provide the raw materials of production and growth in many sectors of the economy and their diversity plays an essential role in maintaining life-support systems and quality of life.

Pressures on biodiversity can be physical (e.g. habitat alteration and fragmentation through changes in land use and land cover), chemical (toxic contamination, acidification, oil spill, other pollution from human activities) or biological (e.g. alteration of population dynamics and species structure through the release of exotic species or the commercial use of wildlife resources).

Definitions

The indicators presented here relate to selected aspects of biodiversity. They concern:

- The number of threatened species compared to the number of known or assessed species. "Threatened" refers to the "endangered", "critically endangered" and "vulnerable" species, i.e. species in danger of extinction and species soon likely to be in danger of extinction. Data cover mammals, birds, vascular plants, amphibians and reptiles.
- Wild bird indices for habitat specialist birds for North America and Europe.
- Selected terrestrial protected areas, i.e. areas under the management categories I, II, IV, V and VI of the World Conservation Union (IUCN) classification. Wilderness areas, strict nature reserves and national parks (categories Ia/Ib and II) reflect the highest protection level.

These indicators should be read in connection with information on the density of population and of human activities and need to be complemented with information on the sustainable use of biodiversity as a resource (e.g. forest, fish) and on habitat alteration.

Overview

Pressures on biodiversity and threats to global ecosystems and their species are increasing. Many natural ecosystems have been degraded, limiting the services they provide.

In most OECD countries, the number of species identified as endangered is increasing. Many species are threatened by habitat alteration or loss, both within and outside protected areas (e.g. on farms and in forests). Amphibians are more threatened than birds and mammals. Threat levels are particularly high in countries with high population density and a high concentration of human activities.

Specialist birds have declined by nearly 30% in 40 years. The largest declines occurred in grasslands and arid lands in North America and in farmed lands in Europe. Widespread forest specialists show fluctuating but stable trends.

Protected areas have grown in many OECD countries, but they are not always representative of national biodiversity, nor sufficiently connected. Actual protection levels remain difficult to evaluate, as protected areas change over time: new areas are designated, boundaries are revised and some sites may be destroyed or changed by pressures from economic development or natural processes. Environmental performance depends both on the designation of the area and on management effectiveness.

Comparability

Data on threatened species are available for all OECD countries with varying degrees of completeness. The number of species known or assessed does not always accurately reflect the number of species in existence, and the definitions that should follow IUCN standards are applied with varying degrees of rigour in countries. Historical data are generally not comparable or not available.

International data on protected areas are available for all OECD countries. The definitions, although harmonised by the WCMC (World Conservation Monitoring Centre), may vary among countries.

For additional notes, see the Annex.

Sources

OECD (2015), "Threatened Species", *OECD Environment Statistics* (database), *http://dx.doi.org/10.1787/data-00605-en*.

EEA (2015), *Common Database on Designated Areas (CDDA)*, *www.eea.europa.eu/data-and-maps/data/nationally-designated-areas-national-cdda-9*.

UNEP (2015), *The World Database on Protected Areas* (WDPA), *www.protectedplanet.net*.

North American Breeding Bird Survey and European Bird Census Council; The Royal Society for the Protection of Birds (RSPB); BirdLife International; Statistics Netherlands.

Further information

Biodiversity Indicators Partnership (BIP), *www.bipindicators.net*.

International Union for Conservation of Nature (IUCN), *www.iucn.org*.

OECD (2015), "OECD Work on Biodiversity", *www.oecd.org/env/resources/OECD-work-on-biodiversity-and-ecosystems.pdf*.

OECD (2012), *OECD Environmental Outlook to 2050: The Consequences of Inaction*, OECD Publishing, Paris, *http://dx.doi.org/10.1787/9789264122246-en*.

Information on data for Israel: *http://dx.doi.org/10.1787/888932315602*.

Figure 1.24. **Threatened species – mammals, birds and vascular plants, latest available year**

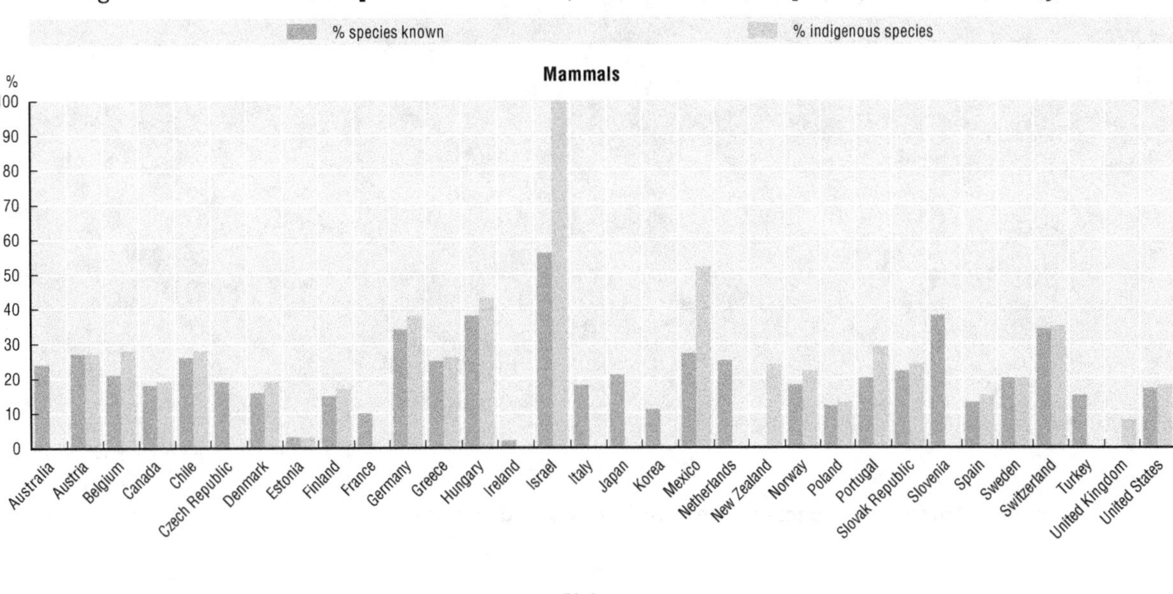

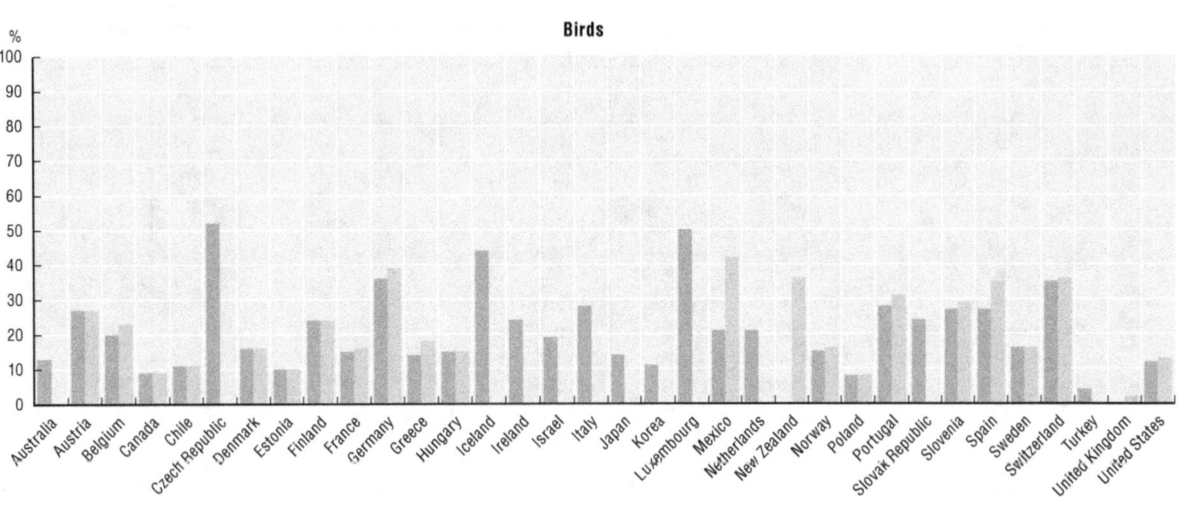

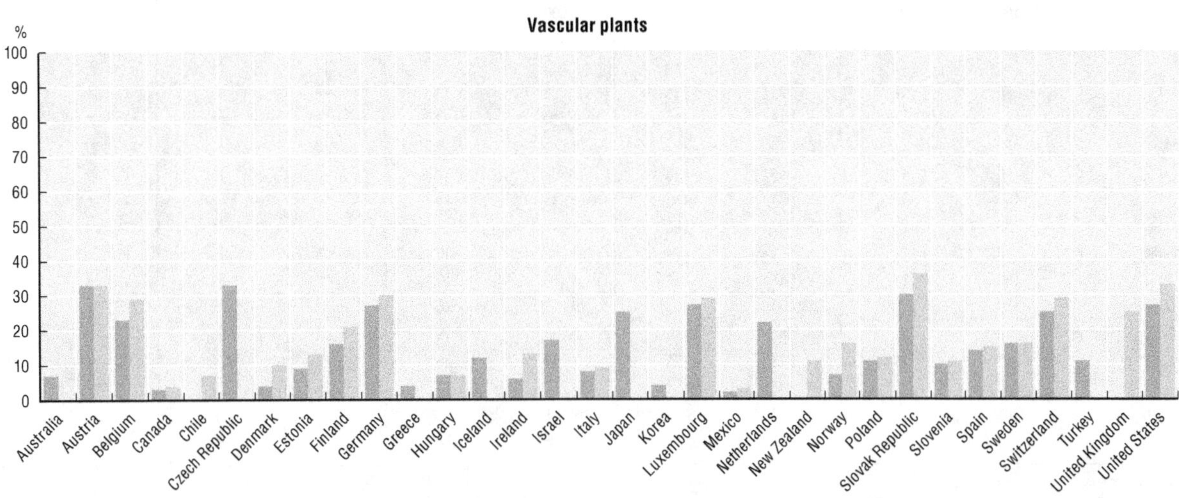

Source: OECD (2015), "Threatened Species", *OECD Environment Statistics* (database).

StatLink http://dx.doi.org/10.1787/888933261914

Figure 1.25. **Threatened species – amphibians, latest available year**

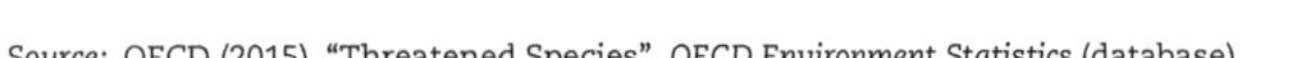

Source: OECD (2015), "Threatened Species", *OECD Environment Statistics* (database).

StatLink http://dx.doi.org/10.1787/888933261928

Table 1.8. **Threatened species – mammals, birds and vascular plants, latest available year**

	Mammals		Birds		Vascular plants		Amphibians		Reptiles	
	Species known or assessed number	Species threatened (%)	Species known or assessed number	Species threatened (%)	Species known or assessed number	Species threatened (%)	Species known or assessed number	Species threatened (%)	Species known or assessed number	Species threatened (%)
Australia	387	24	872	13	19 462	7	226	13	933	6
Austria	101	27	242	27	2 950	33	20	60	14	64
Belgium	84	21	220	20	1 818	23	19	32	10	40
Canada	218	18	664	9	5 111	3	47	34	48	60
Chile	175	26	461	11	..	..	63	57	131	25
Czech Republic	91	19	210	52	3 557	33	22	59	13	62
Denmark	67	16	209	16	2 909	4	15	7	8	..
Estonia	65	3	377	10	1 928	9	9	44	2	50
Finland	72	15	248	24	1 240	16	7	14	5	20
France	100	10	568	15	9 096	..	34	21	34	21
Germany	93	34	264	36	3 272	27	22	36	13	62
Greece	115	25	440	14	5 850	4	23	26	66	14
Hungary	90	38	393	15	2 510	7	18	28	15	33
Iceland	4	..	75	44	438	12	..	..	..	..
Ireland	57	2	457	24	2 001	6	3	33	3	33
Israel	105	56	210	19	2 288	17	7	71	105	33
Italy	126	18	267	28	6 711	8	44	32	56	20
Japan	160	21	700	14	7 000	25	66	33	98	37
Korea	124	11	522	11	5 308	4	21	24	31	16
Luxembourg	..	..	54	50	1 323	27	14	29	6	33
Mexico	564	27	1 123	21	25 008	2	376	14	864	19
Netherlands	48	25	213	21	1 490	22	8	88	7	71
New Zealand	65	..	210	..	4 930	..	8	..	100	..
Norway	88	18	248	15	2 962	7	6	33	6	..
Poland	109	12	453	8	2 933	11	18	..	11	27
Portugal	158	20	393	28	3 607	..	20	10	49	20
Slovak Republic	90	22	211	24	3 352	30	18	44	12	42
Slovenia	89	38	387	27	3 452	10	21	81	24	75
Spain	158	13	368	27	8 750	14	36	31	74	26
Sweden	65	20	257	16	2 192	16	13	31	6	33
Switzerland	87	34	205	35	2 981	25	21	62	19	79
Turkey	150	15	477	4	11 707	11	29	34	129	9
United Kingdom	101	..	272	..	2 951	..	20	..	33	..
United States	453	17	831	12	19 569	27	270	40	345	18

Note: See the Annex for country notes.
Source: OECD (2015), "Threatened Species", *OECD Environment Statistics* (database).

StatLink http://dx.doi.org/10.1787/888933262323

Figure 1.26. **Wild bird indices, North America and Europe**

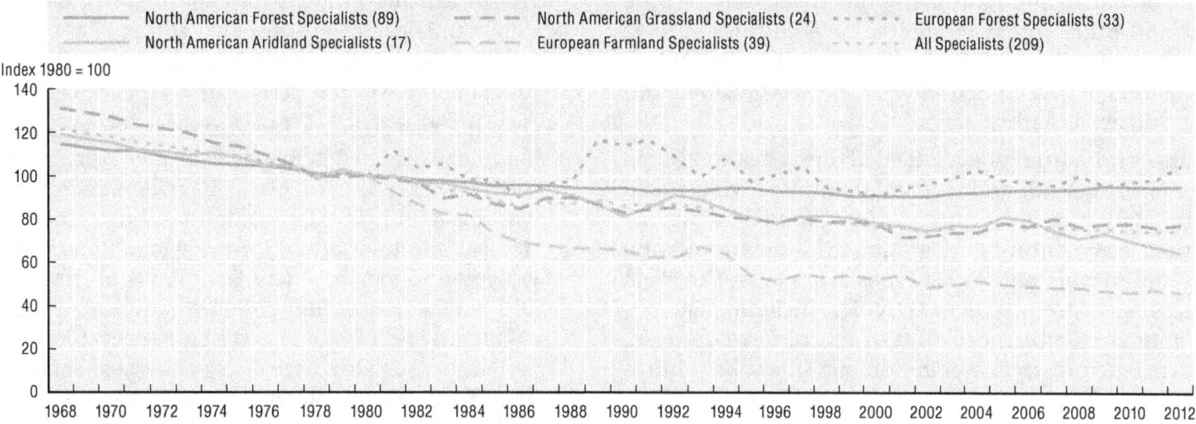

Source: *North American Breeding Bird Survey* and European Bird Census Council; RSPB; *BirdLife International*; *Statistics Netherlands.*

StatLink http://dx.doi.org/10.1787/888933261930

Figure 1.27. **Protected areas, 2013**

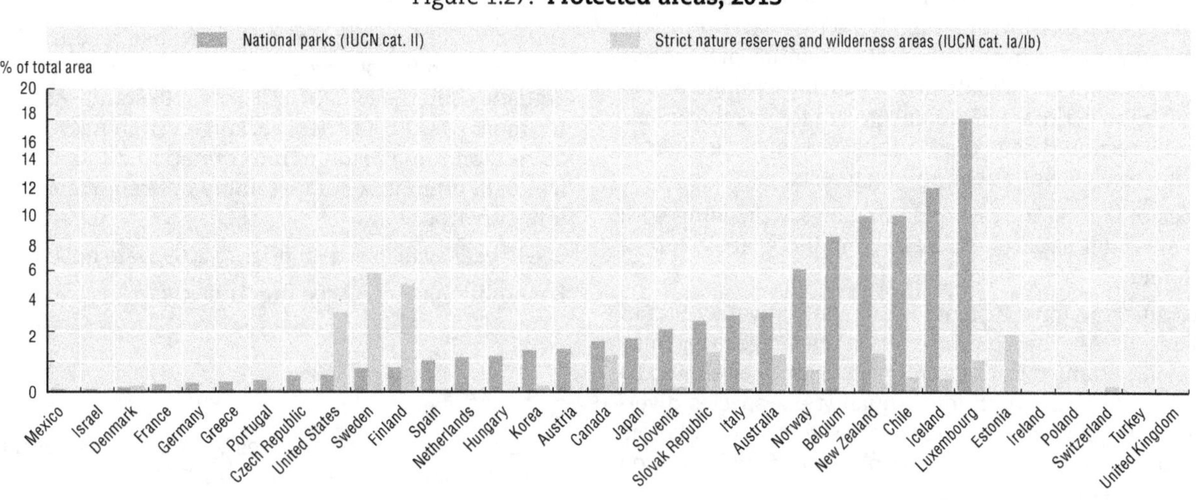

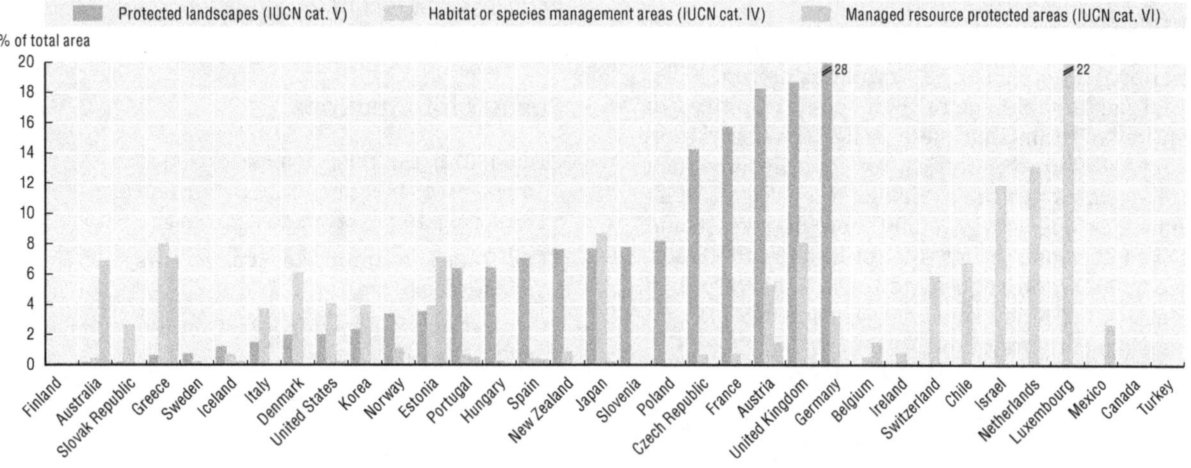

Source: UNEP-WCMC (2014), *The World Database on Protected Areas (WDPA)*; EEA (2015), *Common Database on Designated Areas (CDDA)*.

StatLink http://dx.doi.org/10.1787/888933261946

Use of forest resources

Forests are among the most diverse and widespread ecosystems on earth, and have many functions: they provide timber and other forest products; have cultural values; deliver recreation benefits and ecosystem services, including regulation of soil, air and water; are reservoirs for biodiversity; and act as carbon sinks.

The impact from human activities on forest health and on natural forest growth and regeneration raises widespread concern. Many forest resources are threatened by overexploitation, fragmentation, degradation of environmental quality and conversion to other types of land use. The main pressures result from human activities, including agriculture expansion, transport infrastructure development, unsustainable forestry, air pollution and intentional burning of forests.

Forests are unevenly distributed: the ten most forest-rich countries account for two-thirds of the world's forest area. OECD countries account for about one-fourth of the world's forest area.

Over the past 50 years, the area of forests and wooded land has remained stable or has slightly increased in most OECD countries, but it has been decreasing at world level due in part to continued deforestation in tropical countries, often to provide land for agriculture, grazing and logging. "The Economics of Ecosystems and Biodiversity study" (TEEB) has indicated that the aggregate loss of biodiversity and ecosystem service benefits associated with the global loss of forests is between USD 2 trillion and USD 5 trillion per year.

Definitions

The indicator presented here refers to the intensity of use of forest resources (timber). It relates actual harvest or fellings to annual productive capacity. Annual productive capacity is either a calculated value, such as annual allowable cut, or an estimate of annual growth for existing stock. It should be noted that the national averages presented here may conceal variations among forests.

Volumes of annual harvest and annual growth, along with forest area and exports of forestry products, are given as complements.

These indicators give insights into quantitative aspects of forest resources. They present national averages that may conceal important variations among forests. They should be read with information on forest quality (e.g. species diversity, including tree and non-tree species; forest degradation; forest fragmentation) and be complemented with data on forest management practices and protection measures.

Overview

At national level, most OECD countries present a picture of sustainable use of their forest resources in quantitative terms, but there is significant variation among and within countries. For countries in which longer-term trends are available, intensity of forest resource use does not generally show an increase and has even decreased in most countries from the 1950s. Since 2000, wood requirements to achieve policy objectives for renewable energy resources play an increasingly important role.

Comparability

Data on the intensity of use of forest resources can be derived from forest accounts and from international forest statistics and the FAO/UNECE Forest Resource Assessments for most OECD countries, although differences in the variables monitored result in interpretation difficulties. Historical data often lack comparability or are not available over longer periods.

Latest year available: data prior to 2009 were not considered.

For additional notes, see the Annex.

Sources

OECD (2015), "Forest Resources", *OECD Environment Statistics* (database), *http://dx.doi.org/10.1787/data-00600-en.*

FAO (2010), *Global Forest Resource Assessments, www.fao.org/forestry/fra/en.*

FAO (2015), FAOSTAT (database), *http://faostat.fao.org.*

Further information

OECD (2012), *OECD Environmental Outlook to 2050: The Consequences of Inaction*, OECD Publishing, Paris, *http://dx.doi.org/10.1787/9789264122246-en.*

TEEB, The Economics of Ecosystems and Biodiversity, *www.teebweb.org.*

Information on data for Israel: *http://dx.doi.org/10.1787/888932315602.*

Figure 1.28. **Intensity of use of forest resources, latest available year**

Fellings as % of annual growth

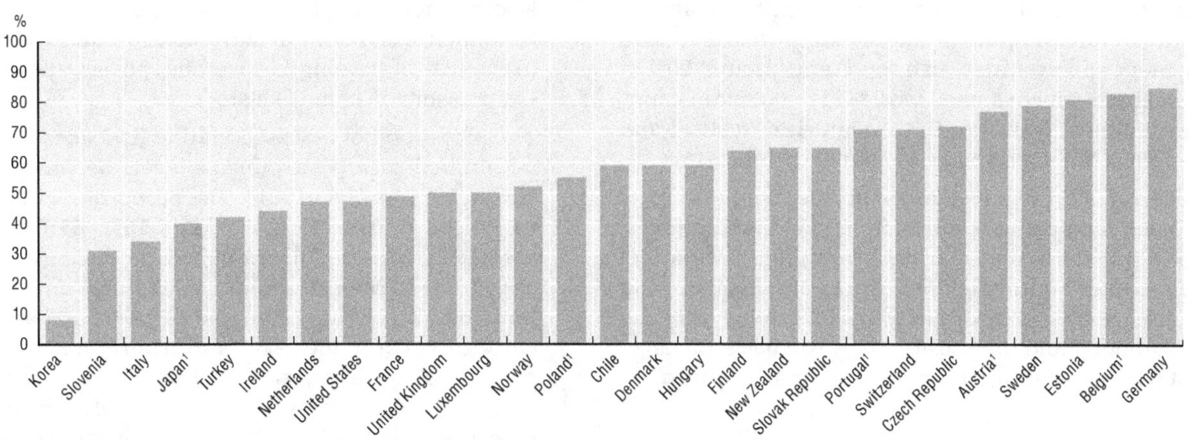

1. Data refer to the mid-2000s.

Source: OECD (2015), "Forest Resources", *OECD Environment Statistics* (database).

StatLink http://dx.doi.org/10.1787/888933261958

Table 1.9. **Forest resources**

	Annual fellings	Annual growth	Intensity of use of forest resources							Forest land	Exports of forestry products
	Million m³	Million m³	Fellings as % of annual growth							% of total area	% of national exports
	2013 or latest	2013 or latest	1950s	1970s	1980s	1990s	2000s	Mid-2000s	2013 or latest	2012	2013
Australia	25.6	..	..	..	..	..	..	..	..	19	0.6
Austria	..	..	..	..	..	66	..	77	..	47	3.1
Belgium	..	..	..	..	..	85	65	83	..	22	1.1
Canada	152.0	..	..	..	..	..	..	..	..	34	4.3
Chile	56.7	95.9	183	..	..	30	45	53	59	22	5.2
Czech Republic	17.0	23.8	60	60	72	78	73	76	72	34	1.6
Denmark	3.9	6.7	85	118	75	36	59	53	|59	13	0.3
Estonia	0.0	0.0	46	41	40	43	|111	57	81	52	5.0
Finland	66.7	103.7	89	101	83	67	73	64	64	73	13.5
France	50.6	102.7	..	..	81	82	..	56	|49	29	0.9
Germany	94.1	111.1	..	..	..	..	75	84	85	32	1.2
Greece	1.2	..	..	..	71	55	..	..	..	31	0.2
Hungary	7.7	13.0	..	60	70	67	62	56	59	23	0.9
Iceland	..	..	..	..	..	..	..	..	..	0	0.0
Ireland	3.3	7.7	..	..	..	..	72	72	44	11	0.2
Israel	..	..	..	..	..	..	..	..	..	7	0.1
Italy	12.8	37.2	88	..	43	42	42	37	34	32	0.8
Japan	45.9	..	..	172	72	55	29	40	..	69	0.4
Korea	10.7	111.9	..	..	4	..	..	2	8	64	0.4
Luxembourg	0.4	0.8	..	..	..	72	..	49	50	33	0.2
Mexico	5.7	..	..	..	23	24	..	..	..	33	0.1
Netherlands	1.3	2.7	..	..	..	55	57	45	47	11	0.7
New Zealand	26.1	40.4	..	..	..	..	54	51	65	31	6.9
Norway	13.0	25.3	88	63	61	62	46	49	52	28	0.8
Poland	37.8	..	49	56	59	50	53	55	..	31	1.6
Portugal	12.6	..	..	..	..	70	63	71	..	38	3.6
Slovak Republic	7.8	12.0	95	64	66	54	56	88	65	40	1.4
Slovenia	3.4	10.8	..	70	64	46	24	29	31	62	3.2
Spain	20.1	..	..	..	..	..	..	..	..	37	1.1
Sweden	84.8	113.5	83	87	81	64	78	85	79	69	6.3
Switzerland	7.4	10.5	..	..	..	..	76	73	71	32	0.3
Turkey	17.9	42.9	..	67	82	52	..	..	42	15	0.4
United Kingdom	10.5	20.8	..	35	32	44	47	51	50	12	0.3
United States	353.8	748.3	78	73	68	84	73	62	47	33	1.2
OECD	..	..	..	..	..	..	..	..	..	**30**	**1.3**

Note: See the Annex for country notes.

Source: OECD (2015), "Forest Resources", *OECD Environment Statistics* (database); FAO (2015), *FAOSTAT* (database).

StatLink http://dx.doi.org/10.1787/888933262337

Use of fish resources

Fish resources play key roles for human food supply and aquatic ecosystems. Fish is among the most traded food commodities, and in many countries fisheries make an important contribution to sustainable incomes and employment opportunities. Fish represents around 20% of the animal protein consumed worldwide. In certain countries, including at least two OECD countries – Iceland and Japan – fish is the main source of animal protein intake.

Main pressures on fish resources include fishing, coastal development and pollution loads from land-based sources, maritime transport, and maritime dumping. They affect both freshwater and marine fish stocks and habitats, and have consequences for biodiversity and for the supply of fish for consumption and other uses. The sustainable management of fish resources has thus become a major concern.

Definitions

The indicators presented here refer to national fish captures and related changes over time. The data on fish captures exclude whales, seals, other aquatic animals, aquatic plants and miscellaneous aquatic products.

Fish production from aquaculture is given as additional information to inform about shifts from using wild resources to more industrialised production. There are, however, important links between the two industries.

These indicators give insights into quantitative aspects of fish resources. They should be accompanied by information on the biological status of fish stocks.

Overview

The trend towards increased global fish catch has been achieved partly through exploitation of new and/or less valuable species and partly through aquaculture. Illegal, unreported and unregulated (IUU) fishing is widespread and hinders the achievement of sustainable fishery management objectives.

Capture fisheries and aquaculture supplied the world with about 163 million tonnes of fish in 2013 and provided an apparent per capita food supply of 19.2 kg in 2012, compared to an average of 9.9 kg in the 1960s.

Aquaculture has been growing and has surpassed capture fisheries as a source of fish production in many countries. In 2013, it accounted for about 43% of global fish production (i.e. 70.2 million tonnes). This growth has occurred more quickly in some regions than in others. OECD countries produced around 8.1% of world aquaculture production with the largest producers being Norway, Chile and Japan.

Unlike capture fisheries, aquaculture offers opportunities to use farming systems and management practices to enhance food production while alleviating pressures on natural stocks. However, aquaculture also has negative effects on local ecosystems, and its dependence on fishmeal and fish oil products, at least in the case of farming carnivorous species, can add to the pressure on some fish stocks.

The proportion of assessed marine fish stocks fished within biologically sustainable levels declined from 90% in 1974 to 71% in 2011. The proportion of underexploited marine fish stocks is 10%. 61% of the assessed stocks are fully exploited, producing catches at or close to their maximum sustainable limits. The remaining stocks are estimated as fished at a biologically unsustainable level and, therefore, overexploited (29%); they yield less than their maximum potential owing to pressure from excess fishing in the past. It should be noted, however, that there is still a large number of stocks for which it has not yet been possible to determine stock status.

Global production of marine capture fisheries peaked in 1996 at about 74 million tonnes and has since declined slightly, to about 66 million tonnes in 2013. The most caught species at global level remains the anchoveta.

Comparability

Fish production data are available from international sources (notably the FAO) at significant detail and for most OECD countries. The time series presented are relatively comprehensive and consistent across the years, but some of the variation over time may reflect changes in national reporting systems.

Data for Denmark exclude Greenland and Faroe Islands.

For additional notes, see the Annex.

Source

FAO (2015), *FISHSTAT* (database), *www.fao.org/fishery/topic/166235/en*.

Further information

FAO (2014), *The State of World Fisheries and Aquaculture*, *www.fao.org/3/a-i3720e/index.html*.

International Council for the Exploration of the Seas (ICES), *www.ices.dk*.

OECD, Work on Fisheries, *www.oecd.org/agriculture/fisheries*.

OECD (2015), "Fisheries", *OECD Agriculture Statistics* (database), *http://dx.doi.org/10.1787/agr-fish-data-en*.

OECD (2015), "Green Growth in Fisheries and Aquaculture", *OECD Green Growth Studies*, OECD Publishing, Paris, *http://dx.doi.org/10.1787/9789264232143-en*.

Information on data for Israel: *http://dx.doi.org/10.1787/888932315602*.

Figure 1.29. **Change in fish captures since 2000**

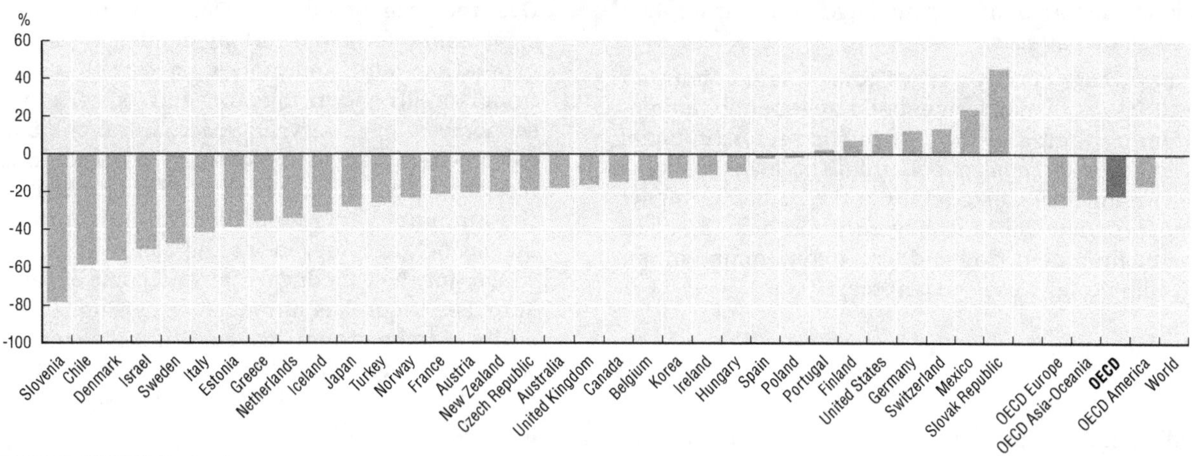

Source: FAO (2015), *FISHSTAT (database)*.

StatLink http://dx.doi.org/10.1787/888933261967

Table 1.10. **Fish captures and aquaculture**

	Total fish captures							Marine catch	Aquaculture production		
	Total			Per capita			Share of world catch	Share of total			
	1 000 tonnes	% change	% change	Kg/capita	% change	% change	%	%	1 000 tonnes	% change	% change
	2013	Since 1990	Since 2000	2013	Since 1990	Since 2000	2013	2013	2013	1990-2013	2000-13
Australia	157	-25	-18	6.8	36	22	0.2	66.2	76	513	140
Austria	0	-34	-20	0.0	10	6	0.0	x	3	4	14
Belgium	26	-38	-14	2.3	12	9	0.0	86.3	0	-69	-89
Canada	852	-48	-15	24.1	28	15	0.9	41.9	172	318	35
Chile	1 771	-66	-59	100.9	33	14	1.9	88.0	1 033	3 084	164
Czech Republic	4	20	-19	0.4	2	2	0.0	x	19	..	-1
Denmark	668	-55	-56	119.8	9	5	0.7	91.5	32	-25	-28
Estonia	69	-80	-39	52.6	-16	-4	0.1	83.0	1	-22	226
Finland	168	26	7	30.9	9	5	0.2	79.8	14	-27	-12
France	494	-20	-21	7.7	13	8	0.5	81.9	202	-21	-24
Germany	230	-30	13	2.8	2	-1	0.2	87.2	25	-61	-62
Greece	64	-52	-36	5.6	12	4	0.1	80.8	145	1 418	52
Hungary	6	-60	-9	0.7	-5	-3	0.0	0.0	15	-15	16
Iceland	1 367	-9	-31	4 243.4	26	15	1.5	98.9	7	149	95
Ireland	246	14	-11	53.7	31	21	0.3	88.8	34	28	-33
Israel	3	-68	-50	0.4	73	28	0.0	76.2	22	51	10
Italy	177	-53	-42	2.9	8	7	0.2	64.6	163	9	-24
Japan	3 657	-62	-28	28.7	3	0	3.9	73.1	609	-24	-20
Korea	1 598	-35	-12	31.8	17	7	1.7	68.2	402	7	37
Luxembourg	..	..	..	..	41	23	..	x	..	..	..
Mexico	1 627	20	24	13.7	36	17	1.8	76.5	169	655	213
Netherlands	327	-19	-34	19.4	13	6	0.4	92.3	60	-40	-20
New Zealand	443	26	-20	99.0	32	16	0.5	92.0	97	240	13
Norway	2 074	29	-23	408.3	20	13	2.2	92.7	1 248	729	154
Poland	214	-52	-2	5.6	0	-1	0.2	89.7	35	33	-2
Portugal	195	-40	2	18.2	7	4	0.2	89.7	8	59	5
Slovak Republic	2	70	45	0.4	2	1	0.0	x	1	..	22
Slovenia	0	..	-78	0.2	4	5	0.0	53.0	1	..	4
Spain	1 034	-7	-2	22.5	19	14	1.1	91.4	224	10	-28
Sweden	178	-29	-47	18.5	12	8	0.2	96.5	13	46	176
Switzerland	2	-40	14	0.2	19	12	0.0	x	1	30	27
Turkey	374	-1	-26	4.9	36	13	0.4	80.1	234	3 945	196
United Kingdom	632	-17	-16	10.1	9	6	0.7	75.0	195	289	28
United States	5 231	-6	11	16.5	27	12	5.6	69.5	441	40	-3
OECD	**23 892**	**-35**	**-22**	**19.0**	**18**	**9**	**25.8**	**78.4**	**5 701**	**102**	**37**
OECD America	9 481	-31	-16	19.5	29	14	10.2	71.7	1 815	341	76
OECD Asia-Oceania	5 857	-54	-23	27.5	11	5	6.3	73.0	1 206	-2	1
OECD Europe	8 554	-18	-26	15.4	11	6	9.2	89.4	2 680	130	37
World	92 587	9	-1	12.9	35	17	100.0	71.5	70 224	437	117

Source: FAO (2015), *FISHSTAT (database)*.

StatLink http://dx.doi.org/10.1787/888933262348

Municipal waste

Waste is generated at all stages of human activities. Its composition and amounts depend largely on consumption and production patterns.

Municipal waste is only part of total waste generated (about 10%), but its management and treatment often represents more than one-third of public sector financial efforts to abate and control pollution. The main concerns raised by municipal waste relate to the potential impact from inappropriate waste management on human health and the environment (soil and water contamination, air quality, climate, land use and landscape).

Definitions

The indicators presented here refer to total amounts of municipal waste generated as well as waste generation intensities expressed per capita. Treatment and disposal shares of municipal waste, along with private final consumption expenditure, are shown as complementary information.

Municipal waste is waste collected by or on behalf of municipalities. It includes household waste originating from households (i.e. waste generated by the domestic activity of households) and similar waste from small commercial activities, office buildings, institutions such as schools and government buildings, and small businesses that treat or dispose of waste at the same facilities used for municipally collected waste.

Waste generation intensities are first approximations of potential environmental pressure; more information is needed to describe the actual pressure. These indicators should be complemented with information on waste management practices and costs, and on consumption levels and patterns.

Overview

During the 1990s, municipal waste generated in the OECD area has risen (+19%) mostly in line with private consumption expenditure (+33%) and GDP (+31%). As of the early 2000s, this rise has been slowing down (+2%). Today, the quantity of municipal waste generated exceeds an estimated 650 million tonnes. A person living in the OECD area generates on average 520 kg of waste per year; this is 20 kg more than in 1990, but 30 kg less than in 2000.

The amount and composition of municipal waste vary widely among OECD countries, being related to levels and patterns of consumption, the rate of urbanisation, lifestyles, and national waste management practices. On average, Europeans generate around 130 kg less than people living in America but 80 kg more than people living in the OECD Asia-Oceania region.

Over the past two decades, OECD countries have put significant efforts into curbing municipal solid waste generation. More and more waste is being diverted from landfills and incinerators and fed back into the economy through recycling. Mechanical and biological pre-treatment is increasingly used to enhance recovery rates and incineration efficiency, and reduce the amounts being landfilled. Manufacturers are increasingly encouraged or required to accept responsibility for their products after the point of sale. The European Union has introduced recycling targets for all its member countries. Landfilling of municipal waste has been banned in a few countries. Landfill nonetheless remains the major disposal method in many OECD countries.

Comparability

The definition of municipal waste, the types of waste covered and the surveying methods used to collect information vary from country to country and over time.

The main problems in terms of data comparability relate to the coverage of household like waste from commerce and trade, and of separate waste collections that may include hazardous waste from households such as waste batteries or waste electric and electronic equipment (WEEE) and waste collected by the private sector in the framework of extended producer responsibility schemes.

In some cases, the reference year refers to the closest available year.

For additional notes, see the Annex.

Source

OECD (2015), "Municipal Waste", *OECD Environment Statistics* (database), *http://dx.doi.org/10.1787/data-00601-en.*

Further information

OECD (2015), "Material Resources, Productivity and the Environment", *OECD Green Growth Studies*, OECD Publishing, Paris, *http://dx.doi.org/10.1787/9789264190504-en.*

OECD, Resource Productivity and Waste, *www.oecd.org/env/waste.*

Information on data for Israel: *http://dx.doi.org/10.1787/888932315602.*

Figure 1.30. **Municipal waste generation intensities per capita, 2013**

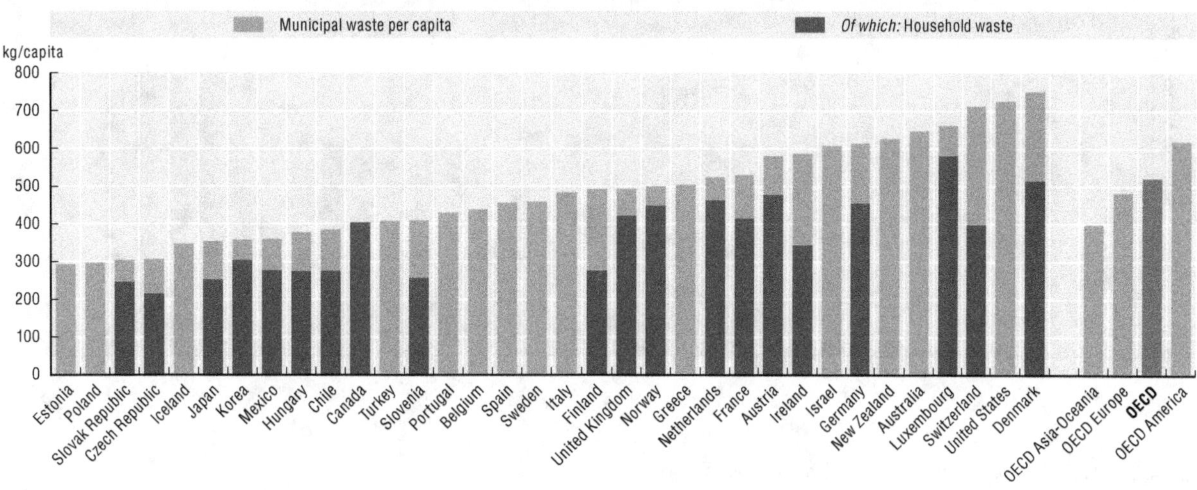

Source: OECD (2015), "Municipal Waste", *OECD Environment Statistics* (database).

StatLink http://dx.doi.org/10.1787/888933261972

Table 1.11. **Municipal waste generation and private consumption**

	Municipal waste generated per capita			*Of which:* From households	Private final consumption expenditure, per capita	
	Kg/cap	% change	% change	Kg/cap	1 000 USD/cap	% change
	2013 or latest	1990-2013	2000-13	2013 or latest	2013	2000-13
Australia	647	-6	-7	..	26	27
Austria	580	39	8	477	21	10
Belgium	438	27	-8	..	20	6
Canada	..	..	10	403	23	27
Chile	385	55	17	275	13	88
Czech Republic	307	..	-8	215	13	29
Denmark	751	..	10	515	18	11
Estonia	293	..	..	..	13	77
Finland	493	..	-2	276	19	25
France	530	15	3	414	19	10
Germany	614	-2	-4	454	22	12
Greece	504	56	13	..	16	-3
Hungary	378	..	-15	275	9	23
Iceland	347	..	-25	..	19	6
Ireland	587	..	-20	344	17	9
Israel	607	..	-4	..	19	23
Italy	484	18	-5	..	17	-9
Japan	354	-13	-18	253	19	13
Korea	358	-43	-1	304	17	42
Luxembourg	661	..	1	581	24	4
Mexico	360	17	18	277	11	23
Netherlands	525	6	-12	462	18	-4
New Zealand	626	-43	-27	..	15	36
Norway	501	..	37	448	28	42
Poland	297	..	..	..	13	55
Portugal	429	43	-3	..	15	-2
Slovak Republic	304	..	13	247	13	54
Slovenia	409	..	..	257	10	14
Spain	455	..	-26	..	17	1
Sweden	458	22	7	..	20	22
Switzerland	712	17	8	399	25	9
Turkey	407	..	..	..	1	47
United Kingdom	494	4	-14	422	27	17
United States	725	-4	-7	..	34	18
OECD	**522**	**4**	**-6**	**..**	**21**	**17**
OECD America	619	1	-4	..	27	19
OECD Asia-Oceania	399	-7	-12	..	19	21
OECD Europe	483	8	-7	..	17	10

Note: See the Annex for country notes.
Source: OECD (2015), "Municipal Waste", *OECD Environment Statistics* (database).

StatLink http://dx.doi.org/10.1787/888933262352

Figure 1.31. **Municipal waste disposal and recovery shares, 2013 or latest**

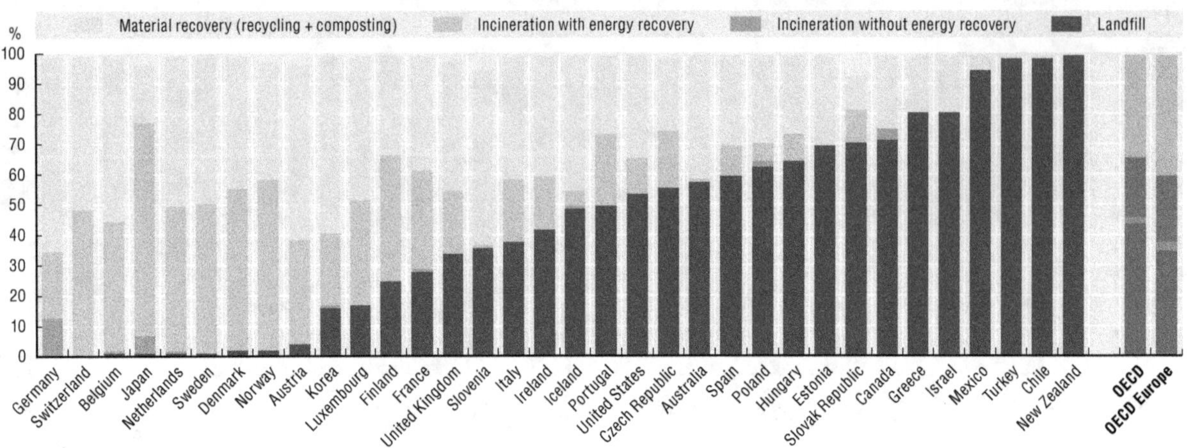

Source: OECD (2015), "Municipal Waste", *OECD Environment Statistics* (database).

StatLink http://dx.doi.org/10.1787/888933261986

Table 1.12. **Municipal waste disposal and recovery shares, 2013 or latest**

	% of amounts treated				% change since 2000	
	Recycling and composting	Incineration with energy recovery	Incineration without energy recovery	Landfill	Recycling and composting	Landfill
Australia	41	1	..	58	..	..
Austria	58	35	0	4	5	-87
Belgium	55	43	1	1	16	-95
Canada	24	..	4	72	21	3
Chile	1	0	0	99	-78	27
Czech Republic	24	19	0	56	..	..
Denmark	44	54	0	2	54	-63
Estonia	30	0	0	70	600	-41
Finland	33	42	0	25	0	-57
France	38	33	1	28	71	-26
Germany	65	22	13	0	16	-99
Greece	19	..	..	81	176	3
Hungary	26	9	..	65	..	..
Iceland	45	5	1	49	150	-44
Ireland	40	18	0	42	263	-51
Israel	19	..	..	81	95	13
Italy	41	21	0	38	..	..
Japan	19	71	6	1	20	-79
Korea	59	24	1	16	51	-64
Luxembourg	48	35	..	17	65	3
Mexico	5	..	..	95	190	33
Netherlands	50	48	1	1	..	..
New Zealand	..	..	..	100	..	..
Norway	39	57	0	2	37	-87
Poland	29	6	2	63	886	-50
Portugal	26	24	0	50	162	-26
Slovak Republic	11	11	0	71	..	..
Slovenia	58	1	0	36	497	-72
Spain	30	10	0	60	..	..
Sweden	50	50	0	1	50	-97
Switzerland	51	49	0	0	36	-100
Turkey	1	..	0	99	-33	6
United Kingdom	43	21	0	34	256	-62
United States	35	12	..	54	25	-91
OECD	**34**	**20**	**2**	**44**	**42**	**-18**
OECD Europe	40	22	3	35	56	-49

Note: See the Annex for country notes.
Source: OECD (2015), "Municipal Waste", *OECD Environment Statistics* (database).

StatLink http://dx.doi.org/10.1787/888933262364

Figure 1.32. **Change in the amounts of municipal waste generated per capita, since 2000**

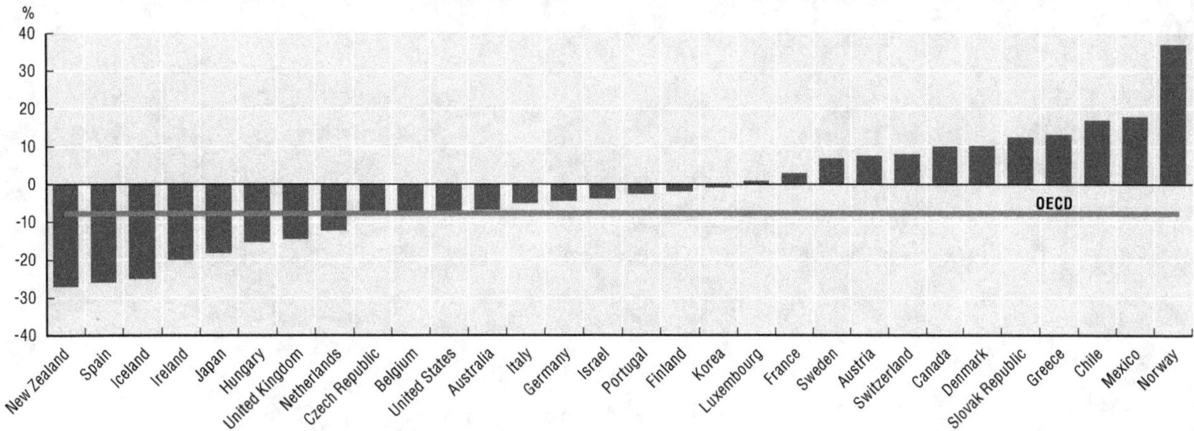

Source: OECD (2015), "Municipal Waste", *OECD Environment Statistics* (database).

StatLink http://dx.doi.org/10.1787/888933261997

Figure 1.33. **Change in the amounts of municipal waste landfilled per capita, since 2000**

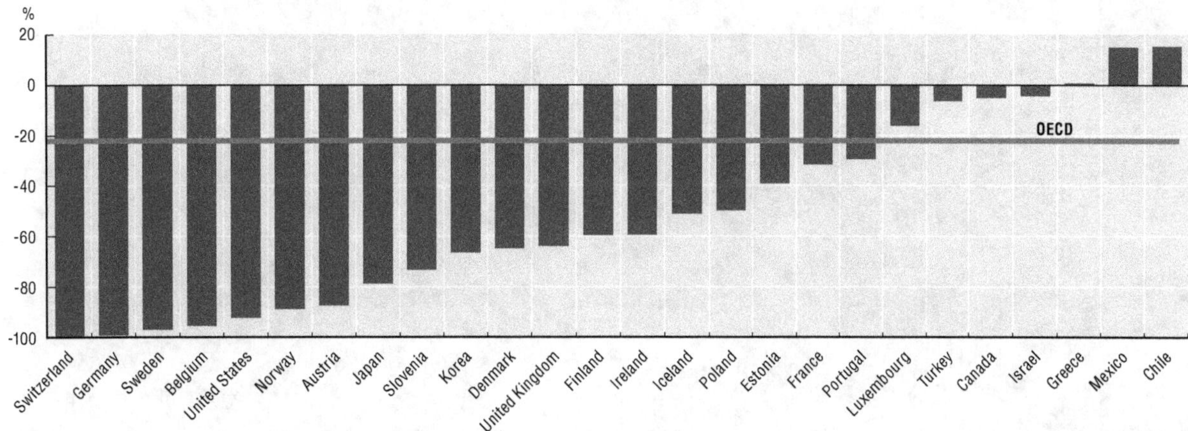

Source: OECD (2015), "Municipal Waste", *OECD Environment Statistics* (database).

StatLink http://dx.doi.org/10.1787/888933262006

Figure 1.34. **Change in the amounts of municipal waste recovered and composted per capita, since 2000**

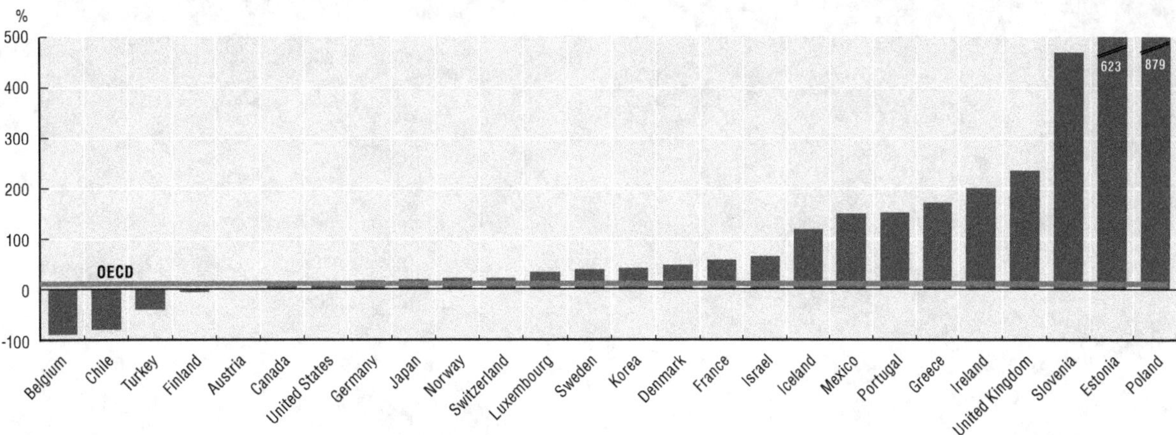

Source: OECD (2015), "Municipal Waste", *OECD Environment Statistics* (database).

StatLink http://dx.doi.org/10.1787/888933262015

2. SECTORAL AND ECONOMIC TRENDS OF ENVIRONMENTAL SIGNIFICANCE

Energy intensity and mix

Energy is a major component of OECD economies as a sector and as a factor input to all economic activities. Energy production and use have environmental effects that differ greatly by energy source. Fuel combustion is the main source of local and regional air pollution and GHG emissions. Other effects involve water quality, land use, risks related to the nuclear fuel cycle and risks related to the extraction, transport and use of fossil fuels.

The structure of a country's energy supply and the intensity of its energy use, along with changes over time, are key determinants of environmental performance and the sustainability of economic development. The supply structure varies considerably among countries. It is influenced by demand from industry, transport and households, by national energy policies and by national and international energy prices.

Definitions

The indicators presented here relate to:

- Energy intensities, expressed as total primary energy supply (TPES) in tonnes of oil equivalent (toe) per unit of GDP and per capita. TPES *equals* production *plus* imports *minus* exports *minus* international bunkers *plus* or *minus* stock changes.

Energy intensity does not reflect energy efficiency, as the latter depends on numerous elements (climate, output composition, outsourcing of goods produced by energy-intensive industries, etc.) that are not considered by the simple measure of energy supply to GDP.

- The energy supply mix, i.e. the structure of energy supply in terms of primary energy source as a percentage of total energy supply.
- The share of renewables in the energy supply mix and in the production of electricity. The main renewable forms are hydro, geothermal, wind, biomass, waste and solar energy.

Overview

In the 1990s and 2000s, energy intensity per unit of GDP decreased for OECD countries overall as a consequence of structural changes in the economy and energy conservation measures, and, since 2009, as a consequence of the slowdown in economic activity following the economic crisis. In some countries the decrease was due to the transfer of energy-intensive industries to other countries. Such outsourcing may increase pressures on the global environment if less energy efficient techniques are involved.

Progress in per capita terms has been slower, reflecting overall trends in energy supply (+16% since 1990; -1% since 2000) and energy demand for transport (+27% since 1990; +4% since 2000).

- Variations in energy intensity among OECD countries are wide (from 0.07 to 0.46 toe per 1 000 unit of GDP, from 1.6 to 18 toe per capita). They depend on national economic structure and income, geography, energy policies and prices, and countries' endowment in different types of energy resources.
- While some decoupling of environmental effects from growth in energy use has been achieved, results to date are insufficient to effectively reduce air and GHG emissions from energy use.

Developments in TPES were accompanied by changes in the fuel mix. OECD countries' reliance on fossil fuels declined although it remains close to 80%, the shares of solid fuels and gas slightly fell, while those of renewable energy rose. Renewables account for 9% of total OECD supply (compared to 6% in 2000), and 22% of total OECD electricity production (compared to 15.6% in 2000). Biofuels and waste, followed by hydro represent the largest shares (60% and 25% respectively). Renewables with the lowest shares (i.e. solar, wind, liquid biofuels and biogases) exhibited the highest growth rates over the last decade.

The growth in renewables was not affected by the economic crisis and was driven by OECD Europe, mostly due to the implementation of policies that promote renewable energy (IEA, 2014a).

Comparability

Data quality is not homogeneous for all countries. In some countries, data are based on secondary sources, and where incomplete, estimates were made by the IEA. In general, data are likely to be more accurate for production and trade than for international bunkers or stock changes; and statistics for biofuels and waste are less accurate than those for traditional commercial energy data.

The high values for Iceland are due to a significant increase in the production of hydro- and geothermal power mainly used in aluminium smelters (+113% between 2000 and 2014).

For additional notes, see the Annex.

Source

IEA (2015), "World Energy Balances", *IEA World Energy Statistics and Balances* (database), *http://dx.doi.org/10.1787/data-00512-en.*

Further information

IEA (2015), *World Energy Outlook Special Report 2015: Energy and Climate Change*, IEA, Paris.

IEA (2014a), *Renewables Information 2014*, IEA, Paris, *http://dx.doi.org/10.1787/renew-2014-en.*

IEA (2014b), *World Energy Outlook 2014*, IEA, Paris, *http://dx.doi.org/10.1787/weo-2014-en.*

Information on data for Israel: *http://dx.doi.org/10.1787/888932315602.*

Figure 2.1. **Energy intensity, 2014**

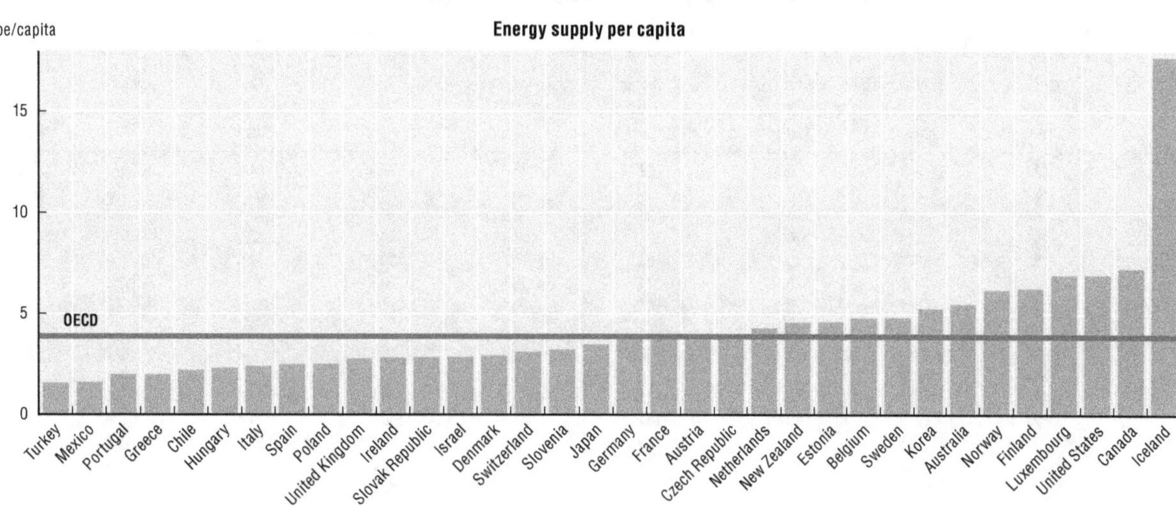

Source: IEA (2015), "World Energy Balances", *IEA World Energy Statistics and Balances* (database).

StatLink http://dx.doi.org/10.1787/888933262029

Figure 2.2. **Change in energy intensity, since 2000**

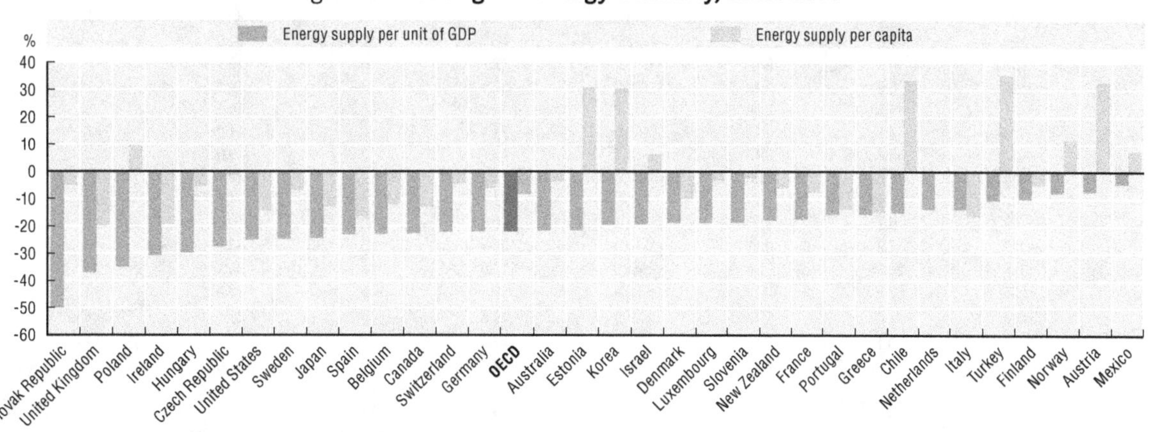

Source: IEA (2015), "World Energy Balances", *IEA World Energy Statistics and Balances* (database).

StatLink http://dx.doi.org/10.1787/888933262034

Figure 2.3. **Change in total primary energy supply, since 2000**

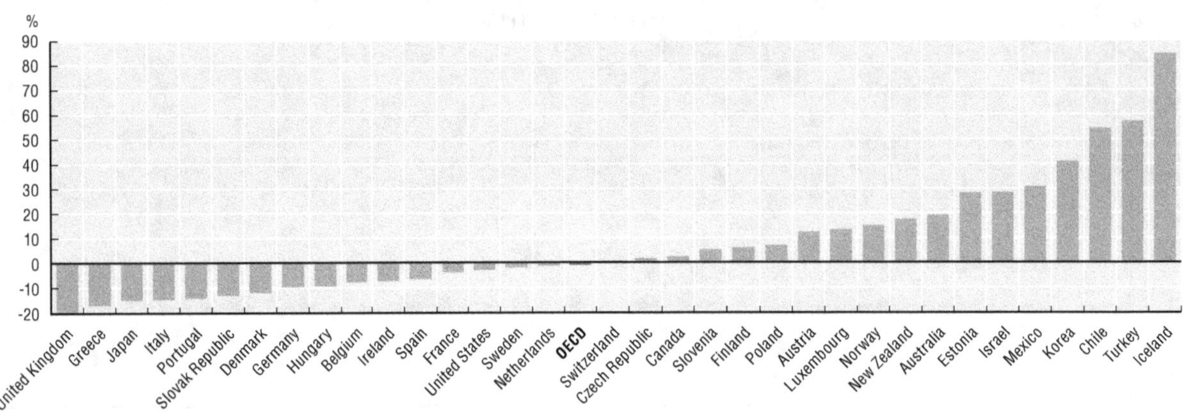

Source: IEA (2015), "World Energy Balances", *IEA World Energy Statistics and Balances* (database).

StatLink http://dx.doi.org/10.1787/888933262045

Table 2.1. **Primary energy supply and intensity of use**

	Total supply		Intensity per unit of GDP		Structure by source, share of the total (%)				
	Mtoe	% change	toe/1 000 USD	% change	Solid fossil fuels	Oil	Gas	Nuclear	Renewables and waste
	2014	2000-14	2014	2000-14	2014				
Australia	129	19.1	0.14	-21.6	33.8	34.9	24.7	-	6.7
Austria	32	12.4	0.10	-7.4	9.7	36.2	20.4	-	33.7
Belgium	54	-7.8	0.14	-22.9	6.0	44.9	24.1	16.7	8.2
Canada	258	2.4	0.19	-22.7	7.4	30.4	33.3	10.7	18.1
Chile	39	54.3	0.13	-15.0	17.7	39.8	10.0	-	32.4
Czech Republic	42	1.5	0.16	-27.5	38.1	20.3	14.4	18.5	8.8
Denmark	16	-12.1	0.09	-18.7	16.1	35.6	17.5	-	30.8
Estonia	6	28.3	0.23	-21.5	70.6	6.7	6.9	-	15.8
Finland	34	6.0	0.20	-10.1	14.8	26.7	7.7	18.9	31.9
France	242	-3.9	0.12	-17.4	3.7	28.4	13.0	45.9	8.9
Germany	304	-9.8	0.10	-22.0	25.5	32.9	20.9	8.3	12.5
Greece	22	-17.1	0.10	-15.6	27.6	49.6	11.4	-	11.3
Hungary	23	-9.5	0.12	-29.7	10.8	28.2	32.5	19.0	9.5
Iceland	6	84.6	0.46	28.0	1.6	9.0	-	-	89.3
Ireland	13	-7.4	0.07	-30.8	15.5	46.8	29.6	-	8.0
Israel	23	28.4	0.10	-19.4	27.6	41.2	26.2	-	5.0
Italy	146	-14.7	0.09	-13.7	9.2	36.2	35.6	-	19.0
Japan	441	-15.0	0.11	-24.4	26.7	43.6	24.4	-	5.3
Korea	265	41.0	0.16	-19.5	30.6	35.7	16.3	15.4	2.1
Luxembourg	4	13.2	0.10	-18.7	1.6	67.5	25.0	-	5.9
Mexico	189	30.8	0.11	-4.6	6.0	51.0	32.6	1.3	9.1
Netherlands	72	-1.2	0.11	-13.8	12.6	40.1	40.0	1.5	5.8
New Zealand	20	17.6	0.16	-17.8	6.8	32.2	21.8	-	39.3
Norway	30	14.9	0.12	-7.9	2.7	38.5	16.1	-	42.6
Poland	95	6.9	0.13	-34.9	52.5	23.4	14.2	-	10.0
Portugal	21	-14.2	0.09	-15.7	12.8	45.3	16.5	-	25.5
Slovak Republic	15	-13.1	0.13	-50.0	21.4	20.0	21.8	27.0	9.8
Slovenia	7	5.2	0.13	-18.7	15.7	32.9	9.0	23.8	18.6
Spain	114	-6.6	0.09	-23.0	10.2	41.1	20.7	13.1	14.9
Sweden	47	-1.9	0.13	-24.8	4.4	24.3	1.7	35.1	34.6
Switzerland	25	0.7	0.07	-22.1	0.5	36.9	10.4	28.1	24.1
Turkey	119	57.2	0.11	-10.5	30.4	26.6	33.5	-	9.5
United Kingdom	178	-20.3	0.08	-37.0	17.0	32.7	33.9	9.4	6.9
United States	2 206	-3.0	0.15	-25.0	19.6	35.7	28.1	9.8	6.8
OECD	**5 238**	**-1.0**	**0.13**	**-22.0**	**19.3**	**35.7**	**25.6**	**9.9**	**9.6**
OECD America	2 692	-0.1	0.15	-23.7	17.4	36.3	28.7	9.2	8.4
OECD Asia-Oceania	879	3.3	0.12	-20.1	28.4	39.6	22.0	4.6	5.3
OECD Europe	1 667	-4.5	0.10	-21.4	17.5	32.5	22.4	13.7	13.9
World	13 555	34.8	0.16	-16.5	29.0	31.1	21.4	4.8	13.5

Note: See the Annex for country notes.
Source: IEA (2015), "World Energy Balances", *IEA World Energy Statistics and Balances* (database).

StatLink http://dx.doi.org/10.1787/888933262373

Figure 2.4. **Primary energy supply by source, 2014**

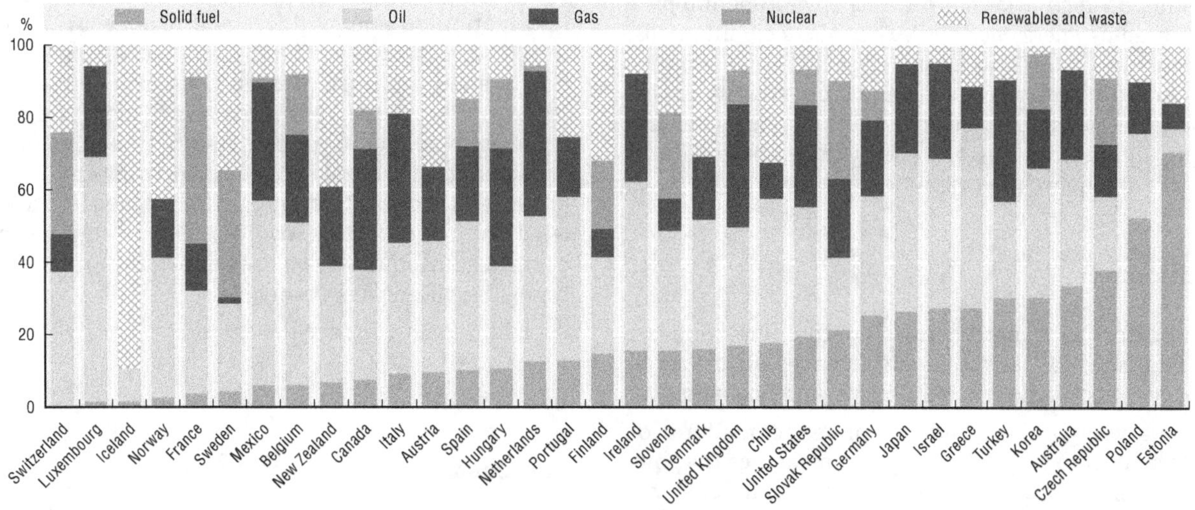

Source: IEA (2015), "World Energy Balances", *IEA World Energy Statistics and Balances* (database).

StatLink http://dx.doi.org/10.1787/888933262050

Figure 2.5. **Share of renewables in TPES and in electricity production, 2000, 2014**

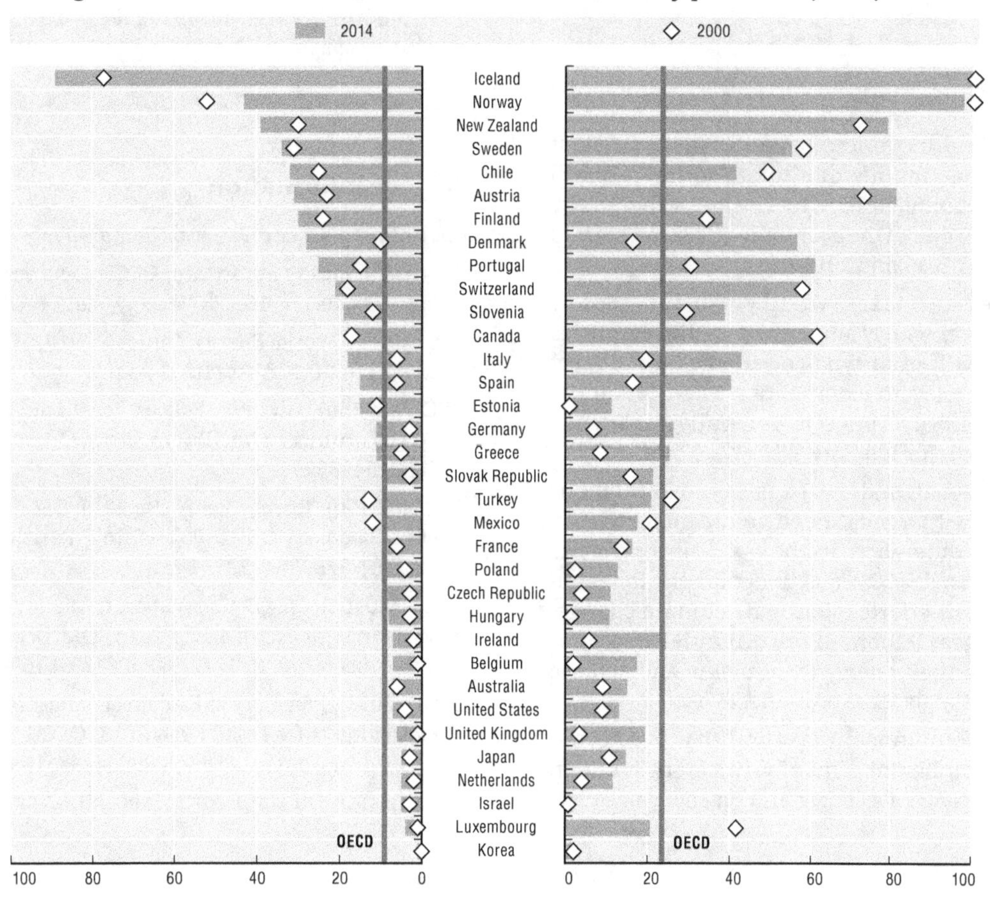

Source: IEA (2015), "World Energy Balances", *IEA World Energy Statistics and Balances* (database).

StatLink http://dx.doi.org/10.1787/888933262064

Energy prices and taxes

Energy end-use prices influence overall energy demand and the fuel mix, which in turn determine environmental pressures caused by energy activities. They also help internalise environmental costs. Though price elasticity varies considerably by end-use sector, historical and cross-country experience suggests that the overall price effect on energy demand is strong and that increases in energy prices have reduced energy use and hence its environmental impact.

Definitions

The indicators presented here relate to energy end-use prices and taxes for selected energy sources (light fuel oil, natural gas, electricity) and for industry and households.

When analysing energy end-use prices, consideration should be given to the various support measures that may provide a benefit or preference for a particular activity or product, either absolutely or relatively. Equally, when examining energy taxes, consideration should be given to the range of energy products taxed, tax base definitions, and tax rate levels and rebates.

Overview

Real energy end-use prices have increased in most OECD countries, mainly due to a rise in crude oil prices; they rebounded in 2010-11 after a temporary drop in 2008-09 due to the economic crisis and started to slowdown in 2013 and 2014.

Energy prices and taxes, whether for industry or households, vary widely among and within countries and between different types of energy, and do not always reflect relevant externalities. The tax component of the end-use price is generally higher for households than for industry.

Uneven price signals and low tax rates and exemptions on some fuels with significant environmental impacts, result in wide differences in the tax disincentives to emit carbon dioxide (CO_2), and underline the fragmentation in current efforts to mitigate climate change. And they suggest important opportunities for countries to reform their energy tax systems and achieve environmental goals more cost-effectively.

Additional information on taxation that is relevant from an environmental point of view can be found in the sections on *road fuel prices* and on *environmentally related taxation.*

Comparability

Information on energy prices and taxes is available from the IEA, but compilation has become a challenge. Deregulation of energy markets has led to an exponential increase in the number of market players and to more and more difficulties in collecting price data on an equivalent basis. Care should thus be taken when comparing end-use energy prices, and the way that energy use is taxed. In view of the large number of factors involved, direct comparisons may be misleading, but may be used as a starting point for analysing the differences observed.

For additional notes, see the Annex.

Sources

IEA (2015a), "End-Use Prices: Energy Prices in US Dollars", *IEA Energy Prices and Taxes Statistics* (database), *http://dx.doi.org/10.1787/data-00442-en.*

OECD (2015b), *Energy Prices and Taxes*, Vol. 2015/1, OECD Publishing, Paris, *http://dx.doi.org/10.1787/energy_tax-v2015-1-en.*

Further information

IEA online data service, *http://data.iea.org.*

IEA (2015), *Energy Statistics of OECD countries 2014*, IEA, Paris, *http://dx.doi.org/10.1787/energy_stats_oecd-2014-en.*

IEA (2014), *World Energy Outlook 2014*, IEA, Paris, *http://dx.doi.org/10.1787/weo-2014-en.*

OECD (2015a), *Aligning Policies for a Low-Carbon Economy*, OECD Publishing, Paris, *http://dx.doi.org/10.1787/9789264233294-en.*

OECD (2015b), *Taxing Energy Use 2015: OECD and Selected Partner Economies*, OECD Publishing, Paris, *http://dx.doi.org/10.1787/9789264232334-en.*

OECD (2015c), *OECD Companion to the Inventory of Support Measures for Fossil Fuels 2015*, OECD Publishing, Paris, *http://dx.doi.org/10.1787/9789264239616-en.*

OECD (2013), *Inventory of Estimated Budgetary Support and Tax Expenditures for Fossil Fuels 2013*, OECD Publishing, Paris, *http://dx.doi.org/10.1787/9789264187610-en.*

Information on data for Israel: *http://dx.doi.org/10.1787/888932315602.*

Figure 2.6. **Tax component of light fuel oil prices for industry and households, 2014 or latest available year**

Percentage of total price

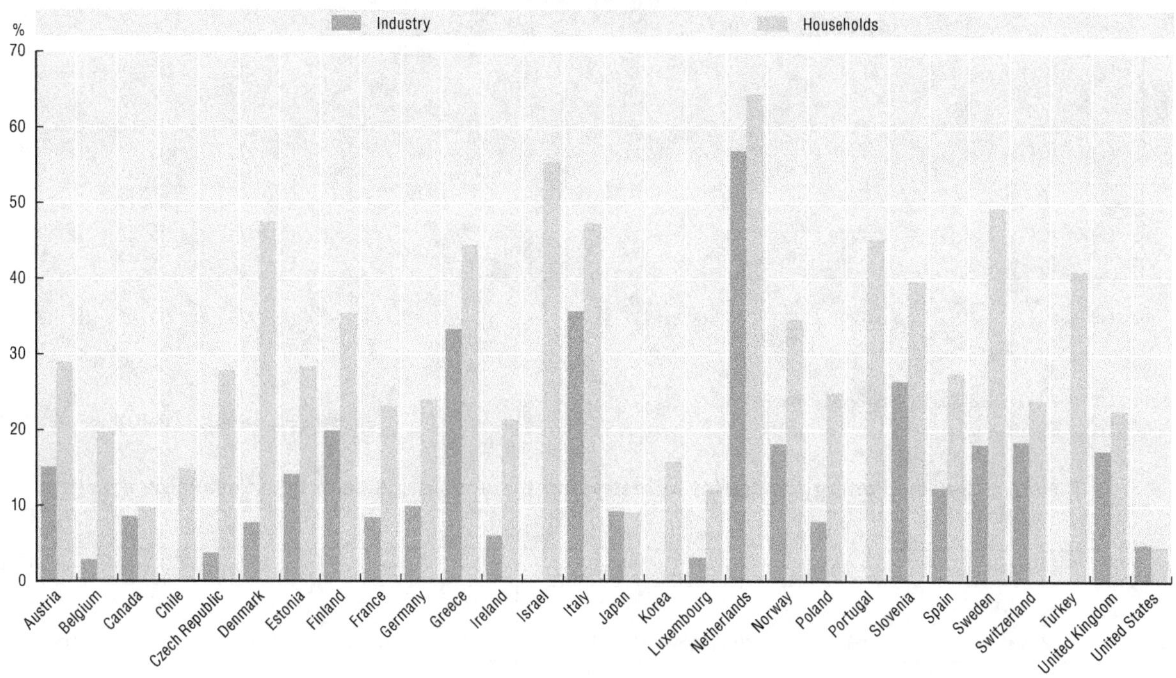

Source: IEA (2015), *IEA Energy Prices and Taxes Statistics* (database).

StatLink http://dx.doi.org/10.1787/888933262076

Figure 2.7. **Tax component of electricity prices for industry and households, 2014 or latest available year**

Percentage of total price

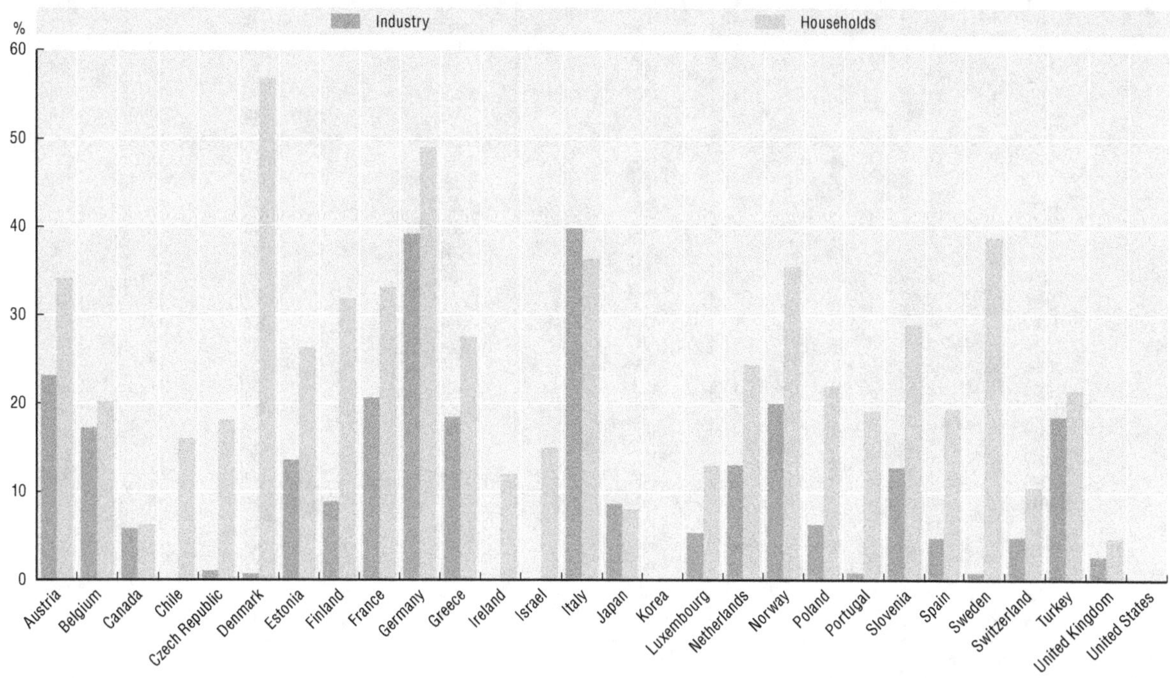

Source: IEA (2015), *IEA Energy Prices and Taxes Statistics* (database).

StatLink http://dx.doi.org/10.1787/888933262080

Figure 2.8. **Tax component of natural gas prices for industry and households, 2014 or latest available year**

Percentage of total price

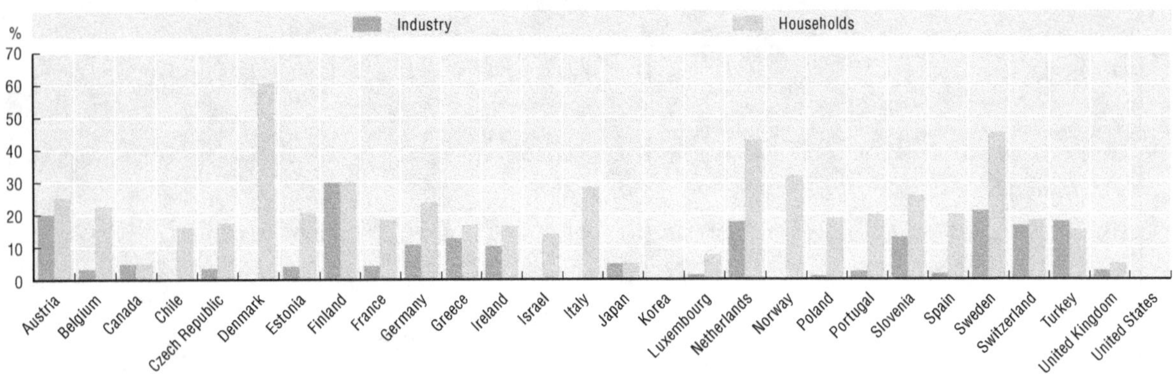

Source: IEA (2015), *IEA Energy Prices and Taxes Statistics* (database).

StatLink http://dx.doi.org/10.1787/888933262093

Table 2.2. **Selected energy prices for industry and households, 2014 or latest available year**

	Industry						Households					
	Light fuel oil		Natural gas		Electricity		Light fuel oil		Natural gas		Electricity	
	Price	Tax	Price	Tax	Price	Tax	Price	Tax	Price	Tax	Price	Tax
	USD/1 000 litres	% of price	USD/MWh	% of price	USD/MWh	% of price	USD/1 000 litres	% of price	USD/MWh	% of price	USD/MWh	% of price
Australia	..	..	..	..	..	..	..	..	..	..	..	..
Austria	961	15	47	20	137	23	1 183	29	93	25	267	34
Belgium	856	3	36	3	128	17	1 036	20	87	22	247	20
Canada	862	9	14	5	96	6	1 135	10	34	5	104	6
Chile	..	..	..	..	118	0	1 273	15	112	16	172	16
Czech Republic	845	4	43	3	123	1	1 126	28	77	17	174	18
Denmark	1 131	8	..	..	102	1	1 987	47	118	61	403	57
Estonia	1 044	14	47	4	118	14	1 252	28	64	21	169	26
Finland	1 091	20	46	30	105	9	1 352	35	213	30	201	32
France	890	8	49	4	126	21	1 143	23	89	18	207	33
Germany	821	10	50	11	169	39	1 021	24	95	24	388	49
Greece	1 315	33	57	13	142	18	1 577	44	140	17	216	28
Hungary	..	..	51	2	123	8	..	..	49	21	158	21
Iceland	..	..	..	..	..	..	..	..	..	..	..	..
Ireland	1 040	6	48	10	165	0	1 290	21	101	16	307	12
Israel	..	..	..	..	121	0	2 039	55	149	14	171	15
Italy	1 500	36	..	..	328	40	1 830	47	279	28	307	36
Japan	915	9	72	5	188	9	994	9	146	5	253	8
Korea	..	..	79	..	..	..	1 234	16	76	..	110	..
Luxembourg	865	3	54	1	107	5	952	12	79	7	207	13
Mexico	668	0	..	..	121	0	..	..	35	14	90	14
Netherlands	1 133	57	43	18	113	13	1 371	64	103	43	252	24
New Zealand	710	0	24	6	84	0	..	..	117	14	225	13
Norway	1 396	18	..	..	55	20	1 745	35	171	32	127	35
Poland	930	8	44	1	100	6	1 185	25	73	19	192	22
Portugal	..	..	60	2	156	1	1 654	45	131	20	292	19
Slovak Republic	1 049	0	44	4	157	0	..	..	71	17	214	17
Slovenia	1 099	26	52	13	115	13	1 341	40	89	26	213	29
Spain	940	12	44	2	149	5	1 137	28	122	20	295	19
Sweden	943	18	55	21	82	1	2 047	49	154	45	214	39
Switzerland	965	18	74	16	134	5	1 082	24	113	18	209	11
Turkey	..	..	39	18	131	19	1 661	41	47	15	170	22
United Kingdom	1 006	17	40	3	139	3	1 025	23	83	5	256	5
United States	718	5	18	..	70	..	1 025	5	41	..	125	..
OECD	**859**	..	**30**	..	**123**	..	**1 116**	..	**64**	..	**167**	..

Note: See the Annex for country notes.

Source: IEA (2015), *IEA Energy Prices and Taxes Statistics* (database).

StatLink http://dx.doi.org/10.1787/888933262380

Figure 2.9. **Selected energy prices for industry and households, 2014 or latest available year**

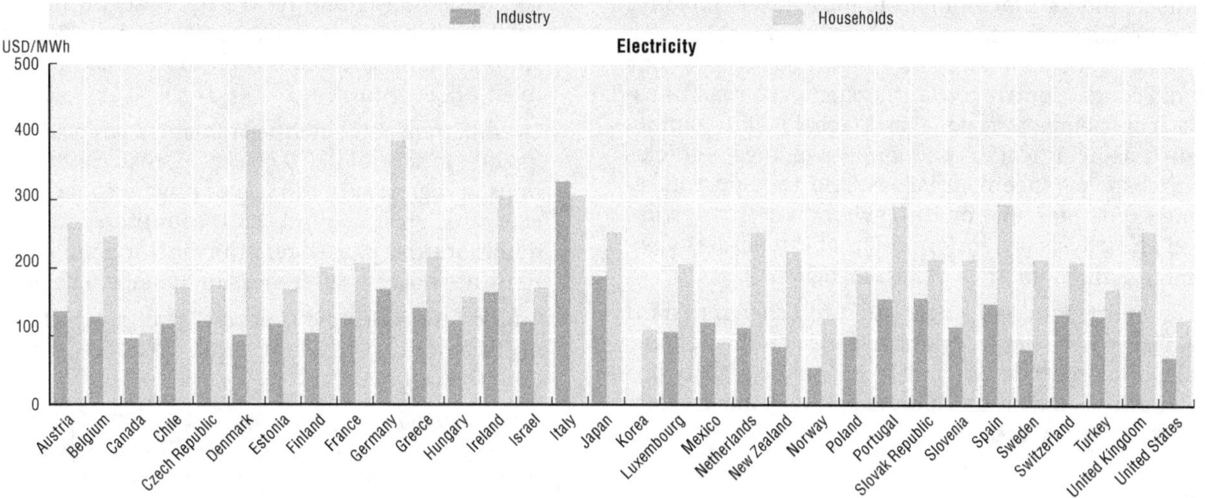

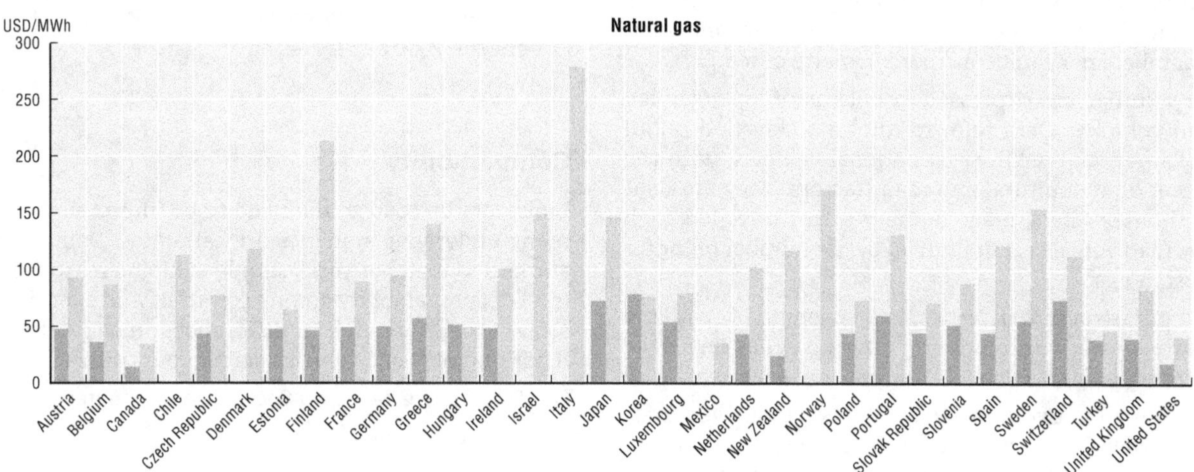

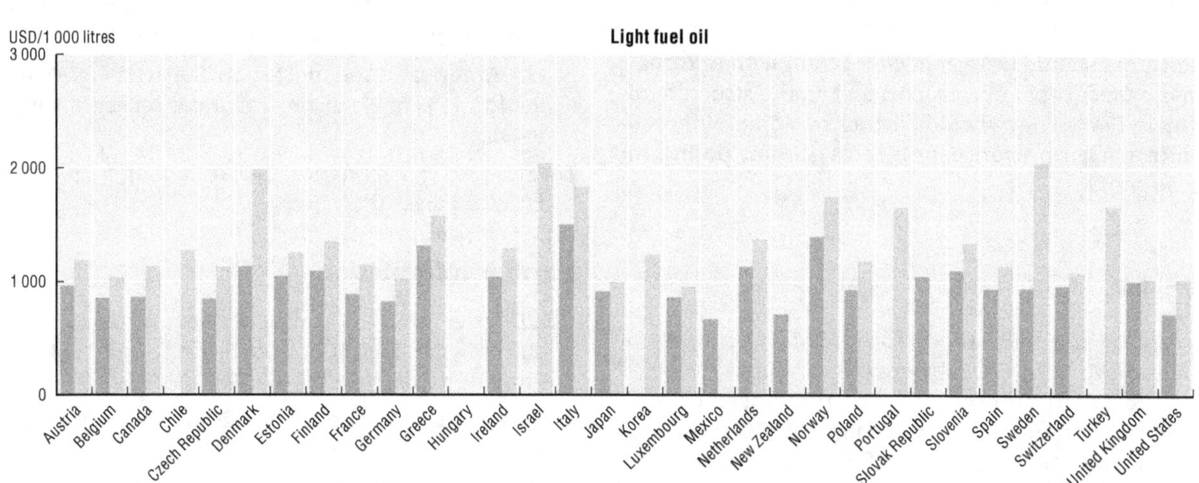

Source: IEA (2015), *IEA Energy Prices and Taxes Statistics* (database).

StatLink http://dx.doi.org/10.1787/888933262106

Road traffic, vehicles and networks

Transport is a major component of economic activity in and of itself and as a factor input to most other economic activities. It has many effects on the environment: air pollution raises concern mainly in urban areas where road traffic and congestion are concentrated, though road transport also contributes to regional and global pollution problems such as acidification and climate change; vehicles present waste management issues; and transport infrastructure exerts pressures on the environment through use of space and physical transformation of the natural environment (e.g. fragmentation of natural habitats).

Road transport dominates compared to other transport modes. The volume of road traffic depends on the demand for transport (largely determined by economic activity and transport prices) and on transport supply (e.g. the development of road infrastructure).

Definitions

The indicators presented here relate to:

- Road traffic and vehicle intensities, i.e. traffic volumes per unit of GDP and per kilometre (km) of road, and vehicle numbers per capita and per kilometre of road.

Traffic volumes are expressed in billions of km travelled by road vehicles. Data refer to total km travelled on all roads on national territory by national vehicles, with the exception of agricultural and road tractors. They are usually estimates: the average number of km travelled each year by road vehicles is multiplied by the number of motor vehicles in use.

- Road infrastructure densities, i.e. the length of road and motorway networks per km^2 of land area. The data describe the situation on 31 December of each year.

The total road network includes all roads in a given area, i.e. motorways, main or national highways, secondary or regional roads, and others. Private roads are excluded.

Motorways differ from main or national, secondary or regional, and other roads, and are characterised by not serving properties bordering on them.

The indicators should be read in connection with information on the modal split of transport and on the structure of the vehicle fleet. They should further be complemented with information on congestion rates and air pollution from road traffic.

Overview

Since 2000, countries' efforts in introducing cleaner vehicles have been offset by growth in vehicle numbers and the increased scale of their use. This resulted in additional fuel consumption, CO_2 emissions and road building. Road traffic, both freight and passenger, is expected to increase further in a number of OECD countries.

GHG emissions from the transport sector increased until the latest recession. After falling from 2007, they were at about the same level in 2012 as in 2000 for most OECD countries.

Overall, transport activities remained coupled to GDP growth. In several OECD countries, road traffic growth rates and growth in the use of private cars exceeded economic growth. In all OECD countries, private cars dominate the passenger transport mode, although there are notable differences in the modal shares.

Traffic intensities per unit of GDP and vehicle availability per capita show wide variations among OECD countries.

Road density has progressed at a slower pace than economic activity in most OECD countries, while motorway networks have expanded at a higher pace. Road density trends are similar for OECD Americas and OECD Europe, but the motorway density increased at a higher rate in Europe, a fact perhaps related to the enlargement of the EU (about +13% between 2000 and 2014).

Comparability

Indicators on road traffic need to be interpreted carefully; many underlying statistics are estimates. Data on vehicle stocks and road networks should exhibit a reasonably good level of comparability among countries and over time, with a few exceptions due to differences in the definition of roads and of goods vehicles across countries.

OECD totals are based on Secretariat estimates.

For additional notes, see the Annex.

Sources

Eurostat (2015), *Transport Statistics* (database), *http://ec.europa.eu/eurostat/web/transport/data/database*.

North American Transportation Statistics (NATS) (2015), *Statistics Online Database, http://nats.sct.gob.mx/english/go-to-tables*.

UNECE (2015), "Transport", *UNECE Statistical Database, http://w3.unece.org/pxweb*.

Further information

OECD/International Transport Forum (2015), *Transport Outlook 2015*, OECD Publishing, Paris/ITF, Paris, *http://dx.doi.org/10.1787/9789282107782-en*.

International Transport Forum (2015), *Trends in the Transport Sector* (database), *http://internationaltransportforum.org/statistics/trends/index.html*.

Information on data for Israel: *http://dx.doi.org/10.1787/888932315602*.

Figure 2.10. **Road traffic intensity per unit of GDP, 2014 or latest available year**

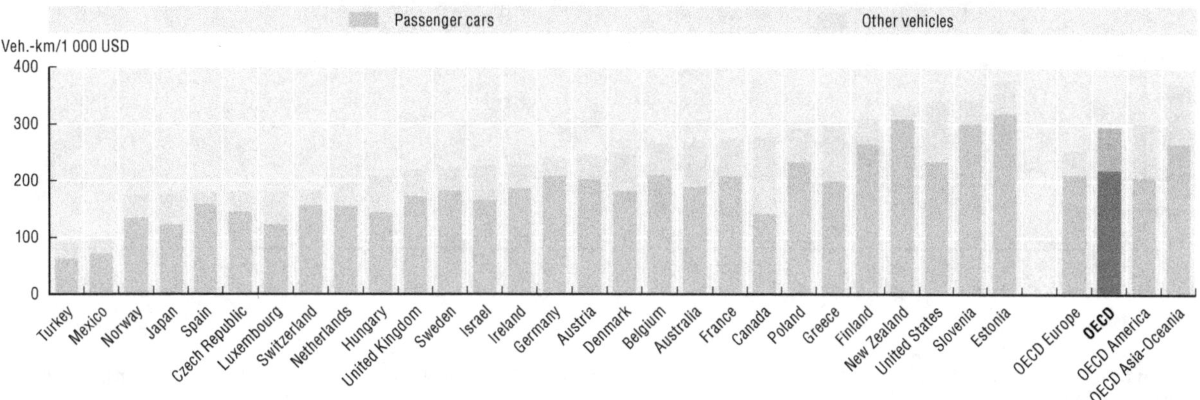

Source: Eurostat (2015), *Transport Statistics* (database); North American Transportation Statistics (2015), *Statistics Online Database*; UNECE (2015), "Transport", *UNECE Statistical Database*; and national sources.

StatLink http://dx.doi.org/10.1787/888933262117

Figure 2.11. **Road traffic density per network length, 2014 or latest available year**

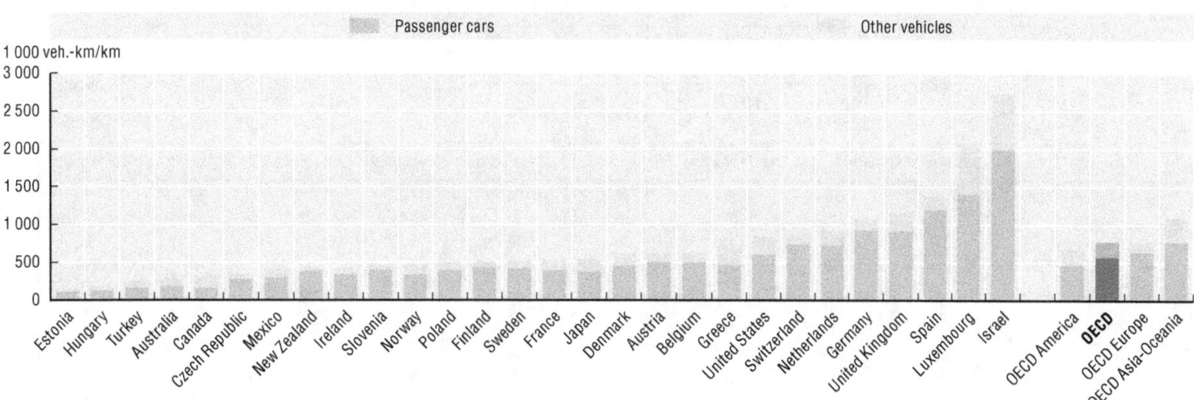

Source: Eurostat (2015), *Transport Statistics* (database); North American Transportation Statistics (2015), *Statistics Online Database*; UNECE (2015), "Transport", *UNECE Statistical Database*; and national sources.

StatLink http://dx.doi.org/10.1787/888933262124

Figure 2.12. **Motor vehicle density per network length, 2014 or latest available year**

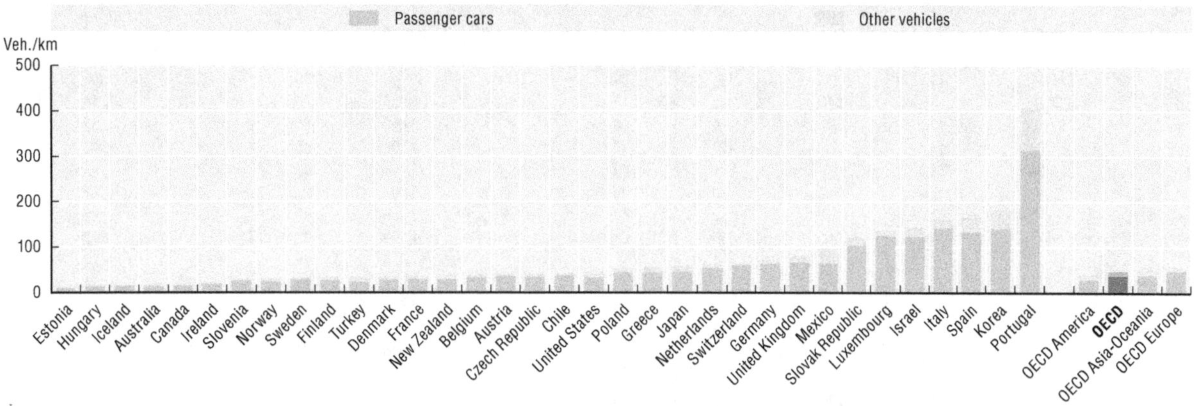

Source: Eurostat (2015), *Transport Statistics* (database); North American Transportation Statistics (2015), *Statistics Online Database*; UNECE (2015), "Transport", *UNECE Statistical Database*; and national sources.

StatLink http://dx.doi.org/10.1787/888933262135

Figure 2.13. **Motor vehicle ownership, 2014 or latest available year**

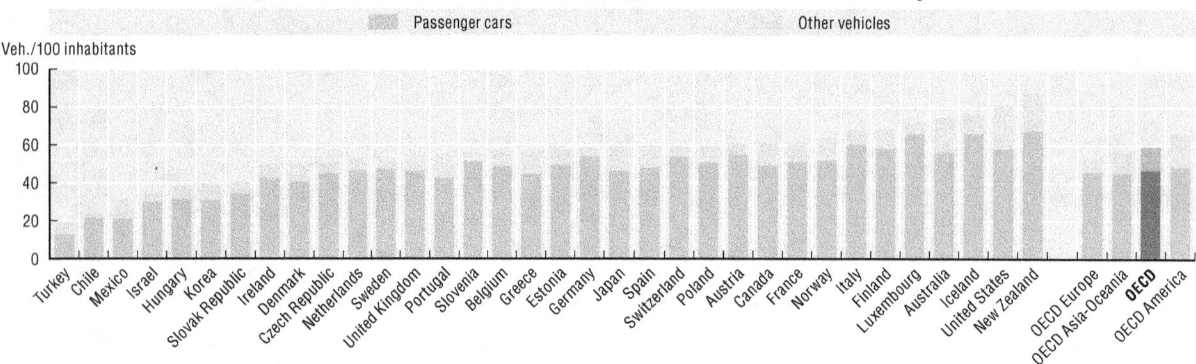

Source: Eurostat (2015), *Transport Statistics* (database); North American Transportation Statistics (2015), *Statistics Online Database*; UNECE (2015), "Transport", *UNECE Statistical Database*; and national sources.

StatLink http://dx.doi.org/10.1787/888933262144

Table 2.3. **Road traffic and vehicles in use**

	Road traffic						Motor vehicles in use				GDP
	Total volume		Intensity		Goods vehicles		Total stock		Private car ownership		
	Billion veh.km	% change	Per unit of GDP: Veh.-km/ 1 000 USD	Per network length: 1 000 veh. -km/km	Volume: % change	Share in total traffic: %	1 000 vehicles	% change	Veh./100 inh.	% change	% change
	2014 or latest	2000-14 or latest	2014 or latest	2014 or latest	2000-14 or latest	2014 or latest	2014 or latest	2014 or latest	2014 or latest	2000-14 or latest	2000-14
Australia	239	30	267	274	57	26	17 633	49	57	11	52
Austria	77	19	246	621	189	15	5 130	15	55	8	21
Belgium	99	9	264	636	38	18	6 380	22	49	8	20
Canada	333	8	278	320	16	8	22 334	27	50	10	33
Chile	..	..	..	..	..	..	4 169	105	22	86	82
Czech Republic	47	16	181	355	0	18	5 330	42	45	34	40
Denmark	46	12	247	615	26	23	2 681	19	41	17	8
Estonia	8	30	378	143	3	14	754	22	50	48	63
Finland	54	16	310	507	12	13	3 766	53	58	42	18
France	560	14	275	532	..	22	38 057	13	51	8	16
Germany	709	9	243	1 081	..	2	46 268	-1	54	2	16
Greece	82	-10	297	698	-47	19	6 456	51	45	53	-2
Hungary	37	59	208	189	42	28	3 778	38	32	36	29
Iceland	..	..	..	..	..	..	246	37	66	17	44
Ireland	40	38	229	429	40	17	2 271	47	43	22	34
Israel	51	39	228	2 730	6	22	2 846	62	30	35	59
Italy	..	..	..	..	..	..	41 321	14	61	6	-1
Japan	694	-11	175	547	-23	29	74 482	5	47	13	12
Korea	1 463	27	989	13 809	17	29	20 118	67	31	82	75
Luxembourg	6	56	181	2 070	51	13	398	40	66	12	39
Mexico	150	140	96	398	185	22	36 742	135	21	108	37
Netherlands	129	11	194	921	11	19	8 956	20	47	14	15
New Zealand	40	12	335	428	-56	6	3 840	65	68	35	43
Norway	44	24	175	462	17	21	3 106	58	52	27	25
Poland	207	50	293	501	-69	6	22 734	90	51	95	64
Portugal	..	..	..	..	-46	..	5 807	22	43	22	2
Slovak Republic	..	..	..	..	146	..	2 196	53	35	47	74
Slovenia	18	34	342	456	101	11	1 153	25	52	19	29
Spain	224	8	180	1 354	..	10	27 456	28	48	11	21
Sweden	77	11	224	527	40	16	5 167	18	47	5	30
Switzerland	61	16	183	854	16	10	4 675	21	54	10	29
Turkey	99	77	93	244	48	27	14 333	140	13	95	76
United Kingdom	489	2	219	1 165	228	19	34 348	21	47	9	27
United States	4 743	8	343	737	31	9	253 639	12	58	23	29
OECD	**12 168**	**19**	**294**	**773**	**19**	**15**	**728 570**	**26**	**47**	**24**	**27**
OECD America	5 500	15	301	679	41	9	316 884	25	49	32	31
OECD Asia-Oceania	2 611	19	371	1 092	5	27	118 919	22	45	25	29
OECD Europe	4 058	23	253	774	22	14	292 766	28	46	17	22

Note: See the Annex for country notes.

Source: Eurostat (2015), *Transport Statistics* (database); North American Transportation Statistics (2015), *Statistics Online Database*; UNECE (2015), "Transport", *UNECE Statistical Database*; and national sources.

StatLink http://dx.doi.org/10.1787/888933262399

Figure 2.14. **Motorway network density, 2014 or latest available**

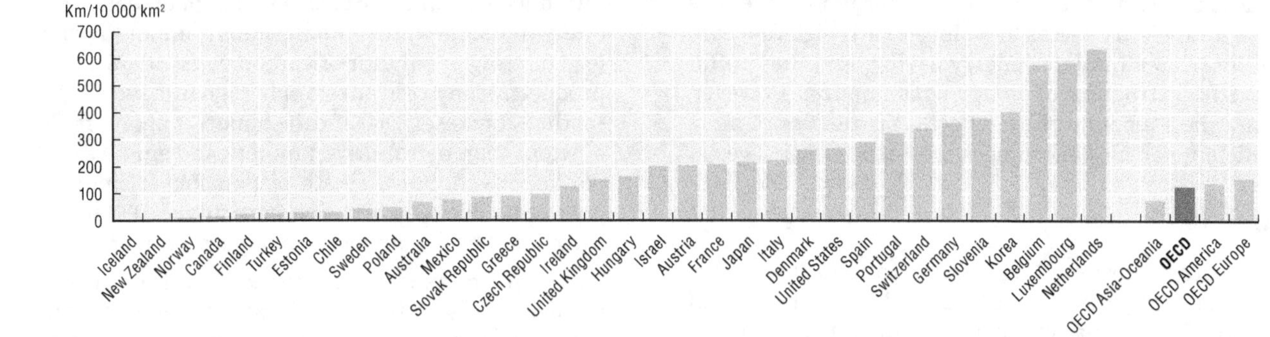

Source: Eurostat, (2015), *Transport Statistics* (database), FAO (2015), *FAOSTAT* (database), North American Transportation Statistics (2015), *Statistics Online Database* and national sources.

StatLink http://dx.doi.org/10.1787/888933262150

Table 2.4. **Road and motorway networks**

	All roads				Motorways				GDP
	Total length			Density	Total length			Density	
	1 000 km	% change		Km/100 km²	Km	% change		Km/10 000 km²	% change
	2014 or latest	1990-2014	2000-14	2014 or latest	2014 or latest	1990-2014	2000-14	2014 or latest	2000-14
Australia	873	8	8	11	..	..	..	..	52
Austria	124	17	16	148	1 719	19	5	205	21
Belgium	155	11	5	508	1 763	6	4	577	20
Canada	1 042	18	16	10	17 000	13	2	17	33
Chile	78	..	-2	10	2 385	..	..	32	82
Czech Republic	131	5	2	166	776	117	55	98	40
Denmark	74	4	3	172	1 128	88	18	262	8
Estonia	59	34	14	130	140	241	51	31	63
Finland	107	39	4	32	810	260	48	24	18
France	1 066	32	8	194	11 465	68	17	209	16
Germany	644	1	0	180	12 917	19	10	362	16
Greece	117	188	2	89	1 197	530	69	91	-2
Hungary	202	574	27	217	1 515	467	238	163	29
Iceland	13	3	-1	13	0	..	..	0	44
Ireland	96	4	0	137	897	3 350	771	128	34
Israel	19	35	14	85	447	..	255	203	59
Italy	255	-68	52	85	6 726	9	4	223	-1
Japan	1 274	14	9	337	8 100	74	22	214	12
Korea	106	87	20	106	4 044	161	90	404	75
Luxembourg	3	4	1	112	152	95	32	587	39
Mexico	379	58	17	19	15 044	172	47	77	37
Netherlands	137	17	5	331	2 646	26	17	637	15
New Zealand	94	2	3	35	183	17	10	7	43
Norway	94	6	3	24	392	437	172	10	25
Poland	413	14	11	132	1 482	477	314	47	64
Portugal	14	-79	..	15	2 988	846	102	324	2
Slovak Republic	18	1	1	37	423	120	43	86	74
Slovenia	39	..	1	192	770	238	80	380	29
Spain	166	6	1	33	14 701	213	62	291	21
Sweden	147	7	6	33	1 927	105	29	43	30
Switzerland	72	1	1	173	1 419	24	12	344	29
Turkey	389	2	-9	50	2 155	667	29	28	76
United Kingdom	420	10	0	172	3 686	16	2	151	27
United States	6 541	4	3	67	263 932	65	47	268	29
OECD	**15 360**	**10**	**9**	**43**	**384 928**	**38**	**31**	**127**	**27**
OECD America	8 040	8	6	36	298 361	72	51	140	31
OECD Asia-Oceania	2 366	14	10	28	..	..	..	75	29
OECD Europe	4 954	10	13	102	..	87	39	156	22

Note: See the Annex for country notes.

Source: Eurostat, (2015), *Transport Statistics* (database), FAO (2015), *FAOSTAT* (database), North American Transportation Statistics (2015), *Statistics Online Database* and national sources.

StatLink http://dx.doi.org/10.1787/888933262401

Road fuel prices

Prices are a key form of information for consumers. When fuel prices rise relative to other goods, this tends to reduce demand for fuels, as well as for vehicles with high fuel consumption. This stimulates energy saving, and may influence the fuel structure of energy consumption. However, there may be a rebound effect whereby greater use of more fuel-efficient vehicles encourages greater vehicle usage.

Definitions

The indicators presented here relate to road fuel prices and taxes, notably the relative price and taxation levels of diesel fuel for commercial use and unleaded premium gasoline.

Information on energy consumption by road transport is given as a complement.

The indicators should be read in connection with information on the modal split of transport and on the structure of the vehicle fleet. They should further be complemented with information on congestion rates and air pollution from road traffic.

Overview

Energy consumption in road transport represents about 88% of total transport consumption and about a third of total final consumption. It has increased in conjunction with transport growth, but the overall energy intensity of transport has remained close to the 1990 level. This is partly due to the introduction of more fuel-efficient vehicles, which has partially offset emissions due to increased usage.

Differences across countries in energy intensity are more pronounced in freight than in passenger transport. Road transport almost entirely relies on oil.

OECD countries have deployed a mix of instruments to address the growing environmental pressures from car usage.

- Standards have been set for fuel economy and vehicle emissions, which have led to improvements in the amount of fuel required per unit of distance travelled, the quality of the fuel, and the resultant emissions.
- Market-based instruments have been applied such as taxes imposed on vehicles at the time of purchase and annually.
- The tax treatment of company cars and commuting also influence transport-related energy consumption.

The use of taxation to influence energy consumer behaviour and to internalise environmental costs is increasing in OECD countries. Many countries have introduced tax differentials in favour of unleaded gasoline and some have imposed environmental taxes (e.g. relating to sulphur or carbon content) on energy products. Many countries apply higher taxes for petrol than for diesel. Diesel-driven motors are more fuel efficient than petrol-driven motors and emit less CO_2 per km driven, but they are responsible for more air pollutants like NO_X and fine particulates ($PM_{2.5}$) and the related health impacts, than petrol-driven ones.

Variations in tax rates and the low levels of taxation on fuels with significant environmental impacts, suggest important opportunities for countries to reform their energy tax systems and achieve environmental goals more cost-effectively.

Additional information on taxation that is relevant from an environmental point of view can be found in the sections on *energy prices and taxes* and on *environmentally related taxation.*

Comparability

Data on energy consumption by road transport and on road fuel prices should display a good overall level of comparability. Care should however be taken when comparing end-use energy prices, and the way that energy use is taxed. In view of the large number of factors involved, direct comparisons may be misleading. However, comparisons may be the starting point for analysis of differences observed.

Sources

IEA (2015), "End-Use Prices: Energy Prices in US Dollars", *IEA Energy Prices and Taxes Statistics* (database), *http://dx.doi.org/10.1787/data-00442-en.*

OECD (2015), *Energy Prices and Taxes*, Vol. 2015/1, OECD Publishing, Paris, *http://dx.doi.org/10.1787/energy_tax-v2015-1-en.*

Further information

IEA online data service, *http://data.iea.org.*

OECD (2015), *Taxing Energy Use 2015: OECD and Selected Partner Economies*, OECD Publishing, Paris, *http://dx.doi.org/10.1787/9789264232334-en.*

OECD (2013), *Inventory of Estimated Budgetary Support and Tax Expenditures for Fossil Fuels 2013*, OECD Publishing, Paris, *http://dx.doi.org/10.1787/9789264187610-en.*

Information on data for Israel: *http://dx.doi.org/10.1787/888932315602.*

Figure 2.15. **Road fuel taxes as percentage of price, 2014**

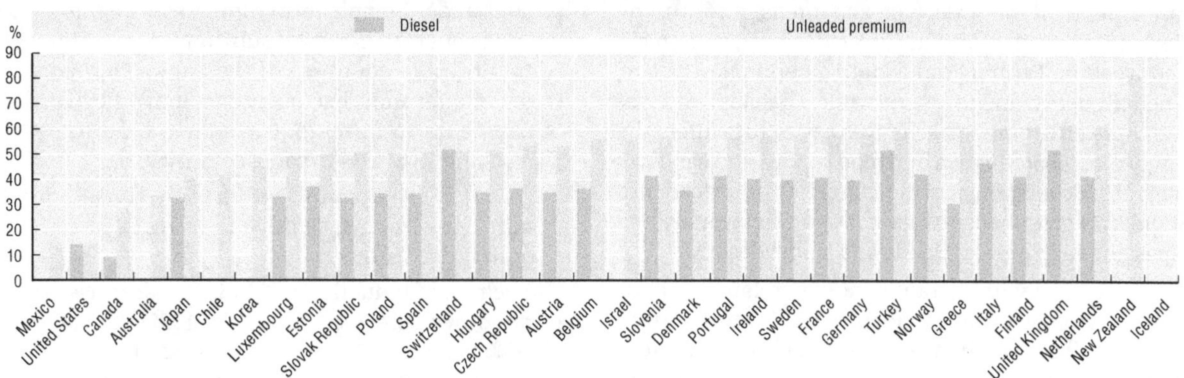

Source: IEA (2015), *Energy Prices and Taxes* (database).

StatLink http://dx.doi.org/10.1787/888933262161

Table 2.5. **Road fuel prices and energy consumption**

In constant 2005 prices and PPP

	Diesel				Unleaded Premium (95 RON)				Energy consumption by road transport			
	Price		Tax		Price		Tax		% of total final consumption	Total	% change	
	USD/litre		% of price		USD/litre		% of price			Mtoe		
	2000	2014	2000	2014	2000	2014	2000	2014	2013	2013	2000-13	1990-2013
Australia	..	..	..	..	..	0.89	..	33.3	32	26,2	16	43
Austria	0.77	1.12	44.7	34.8	1.18	1.27	60.6	53.3	28	7,7	19	42
Belgium	0.80	1.01	44.4	36.6	1.29	1.48	65.8	55.8	19	8,0	0	30
Canada	0.46	0.78	15.9	9.0	..	1.01	..	28.4	25	49,1	5	25
Chile	..	..	..	..	1.11	1.86	46.5	41.7	28	7,4	31	140
Czech Republic	1.54	1.86	40.2	36.5	2.24	2.05	55.8	52.9	21	5,4	-2	-23
Denmark	0.71	0.82	45.3	35.9	1.07	1.19	66.3	57.1	27	3,6	-4	4
Estonia	..	1.61	..	37.3	..	1.78	..	50.0	23	0,7	17	-49
Finland	0.71	0.97	43.6	41.8	1.23	1.37	67.3	61.4	16	3,9	1	11
France	0.82	1.02	54.5	41.1	1.30	1.41	69.8	57.9	26	40,7	-3	10
Germany	0.85	1.21	54.7	40.0	1.26	1.54	69.3	58.6	23	51,6	-3	-7
Greece	0.94	1.16	43.3	30.6	1.27	1.90	52.8	59.8	32	5,0	-17	5
Hungary	1.48	1.99	46.6	34.7	2.40	2.18	60.0	51.6	20	3,3	-4	-20
Iceland	..	..	..	..	..	..	..	..	10	0,3	54	100
Ireland	0.61	1.19	46.4	40.5	1.05	1.34	58.9	57.2	33	3,4	-4	36
Israel	..	..	..	..	1.22	1.64	63.7	56.2	31	4,5	22	110
Italy	0.95	1.30	51.5	46.9	1.41	1.67	64.8	60.7	27	32,9	-6	5
Japan	0.46	0.93	57.1	32.3	0.78	1.23	56.6	41.3	21	64,9	-9	5
Korea	..	..	..	..	..	2.17	..	45.2	18	30,2	32	159
Luxembourg	0.74	0.91	42.2	33.0	0.97	1.11	55.7	49.0	57	2,2	17	37
Mexico	0.66	1.04	31.3	0.0	1.00	1.30	43.5	13.8	42	49,7	20	40
Netherlands	0.89	1.02	49.0	41.8	1.46	1.62	66.4	62.4	17	10,6	9	25
New Zealand	0.48	0.51	0.6	0.4	0.82	1.17	42.5	82.0	31	4,2	2	36
Norway	1.01	0.82	54.2	42.4	1.30	1.40	68.7	59.3	17	3,5	3	17
Poland	1.22	2.01	42.6	34.5	1.92	2.25	57.1	50.4	22	14,8	16	9
Portugal	0.98	1.53	48.3	41.6	1.48	1.92	49.4	57.1	32	5,1	-16	21
Slovak Republic	1.67	1.99	46.7	32.5	2.61	2.04	53.9	50.3	19	2,0	-5	-31
Slovenia	..	1.57	..	41.5	..	1.93	..	56.9	37	1,8	5	32
Spain	0.88	1.16	45.0	34.4	1.25	1.51	59.2	50.9	31	25,1	-5	34
Sweden	0.75	1.08	43.3	40.1	1.09	1.35	67.0	57.8	22	7,1	-8	1
Switzerland	0.72	0.84	63.2	51.9	0.84	0.95	60.3	51.0	28	5,6	5	11
Turkey	1.90	2.78	58.6	51.9	2.25	2.82	61.8	59.1	21	17,7	49	115
United Kingdom	1.16	1.35	69.9	52.1	1.42	1.50	75.5	62.1	28	36,6	-14	-7
United States	0.45	0.78	30.7	14.2	0.47	0.77	24.2	14.6	35	517,3	-3	16
OECD	**0.63**	**1.39**	**..**	**..**	**0.65**	**1.22**	**..**	**..**	**29**	**1 051,9**	**0**	**17**

Note: See the Annex for country notes.

Source: IEA (2015), *IEA Energy Prices and Taxes* (database).

StatLink http://dx.doi.org/10.1787/888933262412

Agricultural fertilisers, land use and livestock

Agriculture's environmental effects can be negative or positive. They depend on the scale, type and intensity of farming as well as on agro-ecological and physical factors, and on climate and weather. Farming can lead to deterioration in soil, water and air quality, and to loss of natural habitats and biodiversity. These environmental changes can in turn affect the level of agricultural production and food supply, and can limit the sustainable development of agriculture. Farming can also provide sinks for greenhouse gases, conserve biodiversity and landscapes and help prevent floods and landslides.

Among the main environmental concerns related to agriculture are nitrogen (N) and phosphorus (P) runoff from excessive fertiliser use, intensive livestock farming and pesticides. N and P, while major plant nutrients, are responsible for water eutrophication and related effects on aquatic life and water quality. Nitrogen further increases soil acidification, contributes to air pollution and alters the balance of greenhouse gases. The main challenge is to progressively decrease the negative and increase the positive environmental effects of agricultural production so that ecosystem functions can be maintained and food security ensured for the world's population.

Definitions

The indicators presented here relate to:

- The intensity of use of commercial fertilisers, expressed as the apparent consumption of nitrogen and phosphate fertilisers (in active ingredients), per hectare of agricultural land.
- Livestock densities, expressed as the number of live animals (in sheep equivalent heads) per hectare of agricultural land.

The share of agricultural land under organic farming, changes in agricultural production and in agricultural land are given as complements. They reflect drivers of farm input use: nutrients, pesticides, energy and water, etc.

These indicators describe potential, not actual, environmental pressures, and may hide important spatial variations. They should be read with information on agricultural nutrient balances, water use in agriculture, soil quality, biodiversity and farm management.

Overview

The economic and social significance of the agricultural sector has been declining in most OECD countries for decades. During the 2000s, growth in OECD agricultural production has been slowing compared to the 1990s, and in nearly all OECD countries, the land area used for agricultural purposes has decreased. It has been mainly converted to use for forestry and urban development. Nevertheless, for almost two-thirds of OECD countries, agriculture remains the major land use, representing over 40% of total land area. The share of agricultural land under organic farming remains very low, around 2%, though this masks substantial variations across countries. In countries of the European Union, where organic farming has been encouraged by conversion payments to farmers, the shares tend to be higher reaching 10 to 17% in some countries.

For many OECD countries, fertiliser consumption and nutrient surpluses relative to changes in agricultural output declined.

The rate of reduction in OECD fertiliser use was more rapid over the 2000s than the 1990s. Since the early 2000s, the OECD volume of agricultural production increased by more than 3%, whereas the intensity of use of phosphate fertilisers declined by 9% and that of nitrogenous fertilisers grew by 12%. It reflects both improvements in nutrient use efficiency by farmers and slower growth in agricultural output for many countries over the 2000s.

There are, however, sizeable variations within and between countries in terms of fertiliser use. Territorial variations within countries are explained by the spatial distribution of intensive livestock farming and cropping systems that require high nutrient inputs, such as maize and rice.

Comparability

Cross-country comparisons of changes over time should take into account the absolute levels during the reference period.

Fertiliser, agricultural land use and production data are generally of good quality. Some caution is required in interpreting the indicators related to organic farming; the definition of what constitutes organic farming may differ across countries. Data on livestock densities are estimated based on livestock numbers and coefficients to convert to sheep equivalents.

For additional notes, see the Annex.

Source

FAO (2015), FAOSTAT (database), *http://faostat3.fao.org*.

Further information

OECD/FAO (2015), *OECD-FAO Agricultural Outlook 2015*, OECD Publishing, Paris, *http://dx.doi.org/10.1787/agr_outlook-2015-en*.

OECD (2013), *OECD Compendium of Agri-Environmental Indicators*, OECD Publishing, Paris, *http://dx.doi.org/10.1787/9789264186217-en*.

OECD (2013), "Agri-Environmental Indicators: Environmental Performance of Agriculture 2013", *OECD Agriculture Statistics* (database), *http://dx.doi.org/10.1787/data-00660-en*.

Information on data for Israel: *http://dx.doi.org/10.1787/888932315602*.

Figure 2.16. **Intensity of use of nitrogen and phosphate fertilisers, kg per hectare of agricultural land**

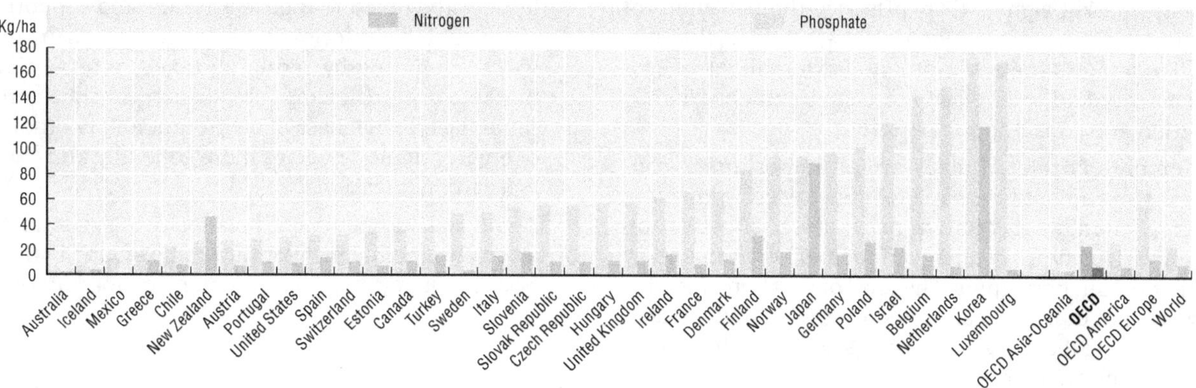

Source: FAO (2015), *FAOSTAT* (database); Eurostat (2015), *Agriculture Statistics* (database).

StatLink http://dx.doi.org/10.1787/888933262174

Table 2.6. **Fertiliser use, livestock and agricultural land**

	Intensity of use of commercial fertilisers: Apparent consumption per hectare of agricultural land – Nitrogen		Phosphates		Livestock density: Live animals per unit of agricultural land		Agricultural land: As a share of total area		Organic farming: As a share of agricultural land	Agricultural production
	(Kg/ha)	% change	(Kg/ha)	% change	Heads/km^2	% change	%	% change	%	% change
	2012	Since 2002	2012	Since 2002	2012	Since 2000	2012	Since 2000	2012	Since 2000
Australia	3	24	2	-17	65	0	52	-11	3.0	9.2
Austria	27	-46	7	-68	525	-10	38	-7	17.0	2.5
Belgium	143	12	17	-55	1 788	-245	44	-4	4.5	-5.0
Canada	36	47	11	14	152	-3	7	-3	1.3	23.8
Chile	22	37	8	-23	210	-32	21	5	0.1	41.5
Czech Republic	56	24	10	8	273	-60	54	-1	11.3	-9.8
Denmark	67	13	13	531	879	-57	61	-1	6.7	2.9
Estonia	34	44	7	23	227	16	21	-3	15.1	25.3
Finland	84	5	32	47	337	-47	7	3	8.7	0.4
France	66	-11	9	-64	526	-35	53	-3	3.6	-6.7
Germany	99	-6	17	-12	709	-29	47	-2	6.2	3.2
Greece	17	-47	11	-22	263	10	62	-4	5.7	-19.4
Hungary	57	9	12	9	216	-20	57	-9	2.4	-5.1
Iceland	5	-14	4	50	68	-2	18	-1	1.0	18.9
Ireland	62	-42	17	-26	1 095	-50	64	3	1.2	-5.2
Israel	122	54	23	10	1 210	322	24	-8	1.1	26.1
Italy	50	-10	15	-27	490	18	46	-12	8.5	-9.8
Japan	95	-15	90	-33	1 156	105	12	-14	0.2	-5.5
Korea	169	-11	119	57	2 243	825	18	-10	1.4	0.2
Luxembourg	171	-16	6	-84	983	-63	51	3	3.1	-14.0
Mexico	13	53	1	-75	302	22	54	0	0.5	31.2
Netherlands	151	1	8	-67	2 404	55	44	-6	2.6	6.0
New Zealand	27	5	46	38	828	192	42	-27	0.9	23.0
Norway	95	0	19	-29	874	-31	3	-5	5.6	2.6
Poland	103	108	27	51	386	60	46	-21	4.6	4.1
Portugal	28	-34	10	-50	471	-14	39	-5	5.5	2.6
Slovak Republic	56	53	11	37	241	-35	39	-21	8.6	-3.6
Slovenia	54	-17	18	-38	732	-5	24	-7	7.3	-16.4
Spain	31	-10	14	-32	331	7	53	-10	6.4	9.7
Sweden	49	-17	3	-72	391	-31	7	-3	15.7	-7.8
Switzerland	32	22	11	4	808	30	37	-2	7.9	-1.1
Turkey	38	32	16	39	357	49	49	-5	1.8	32.1
United Kingdom	58	-17	11	-30	630	-120	71	1	3.4	-3.8
United States	30	12	10	0	193	-3	42	-3	0.5	12.7
OECD	**25**	**12**	**8**	**-9**	**220**	**5**	**34**	**-6**	**2.2**	..
OECD America	27	19	8	-5	208	1	26	-2	0.6	..
OECD Asia-Oceania	5	9	5	-5	106	7	50	-11	2.9	..
OECD Europe	63	2	16	-18	490	-1	39	-7	5.6	..
World	24	39	9	37	305	42	37	0	..	37.2

Note: See the Annex for country notes.

Source: FAO (2015), *FAOSTAT* (database).

StatLink http://dx.doi.org/10.1787/888933262429

Environmentally related taxation

Prices and financial transfers (taxes, subsidies) provide important market signals that influence the behaviour of producers and consumers. Along with regulations, they can be used to address the environmental externalities of economic activity and to leverage more environment-friendly production and consumption patterns.

Environmentally related taxes are an important instrument for governments to shape relative prices. In the case of energy, changes in relative price affect substitution between various types of energy input and between energy and other production inputs. The level of taxation of energy relative to that of labour can influence the relative price of inputs, affect labour demand and stimulate the use of energy from cleaner sources.

Definitions

The indicators presented here refer to:

- Environmentally related tax revenue, expressed as percentage of GDP and as percentage of total tax revenue.
- The structure of the environmentally related tax base, i.e. energy products, motor vehicles and transport, and others (e.g. waste management, water management, ozone-depleting substances).

Overview

The use of environmentally related taxes to influence consumer behaviour and to internalise environmental costs is growing in OECD countries, but remains limited compared to labour taxes.

The revenue raised by environmentally related taxes represents about 1.6% of GDP, and 5.2% of all tax revenue. Both of these shares decreased slightly over the past decade, in part due to rising international fuel prices that triggered substitution away from motor vehicle fuels, some of the most heavily taxed products in the economy.

In OECD countries, the structure of environmentally related tax revenue is dominated by taxes on energy products, including motor vehicle fuels (69%) and on motor vehicles and transport (28%). Other environmentally related taxes, such as those on waste and water management and on hazardous chemicals – for which the price elasticities in many cases are larger than for energy and vehicles – represent a relatively low though growing share in current tax revenue (3%).

It has to be noted that governments also support fossil energy production and consumption in many ways, including by reducing taxes, intervening in markets or transferring funds. Such subsidies undermine the effectiveness of environmental taxation and of environmental policies more generally and encourage carbon emissions.

Additional information on taxation that is relevant from an environmental point of view can be found in the sections on energy prices and taxes and on road fuel prices.

Comparability

The indicators on environmentally related taxes should not be used to judge the "environment friendliness" of the tax systems. For such analysis, additional information, describing the economic and taxation structure of each country, is required. It should also be kept in mind that revenue from fees and charges, and from levies related to resource management, is not included, except for charges whose benefits are in proportion with their payment (e.g. wastewater charges).

For additional notes, see the Annex.

Sources

OECD (2014), "Environmental Policy Instruments", *OECD Environment Statistics* (database), *http://dx.doi.org/10.1787/data-00696-en*.

OECD (2014), "Revenue Statistics: Comparative Tables", *OECD Tax Statistics* (database), *http://dx.doi.org/10.1787/data-00262-en*.

Further information

OECD (2015), *Database on Instruments Used for Environmental Policy and Natural Resources Management, www2.oecd.org/ecoinst/queries/Default.aspx*.

OECD (2014), "Green Growth Indicators 2014", *OECD Green Growth Studies*, OECD Publishing, Paris, *http://dx.doi.org/10.1787/9789264202030-en*.

Information on data for Israel: *http://dx.doi.org/10.1787/888932315602*.

Figure 2.17. **Environmentally related tax revenue**

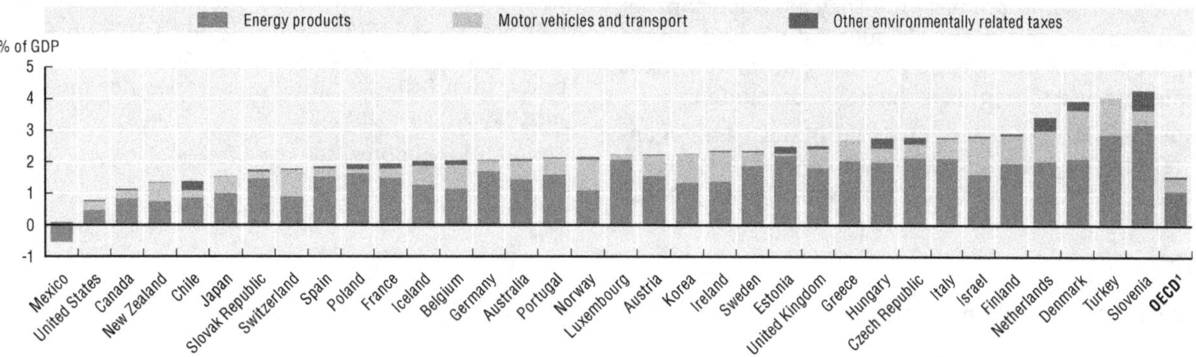

Note: Since 2000, Mexico has applied a price-smoothing mechanism. If petrol and diesel prices are higher than international reference prices, the differential effectively represents an excise duty, known as the *Impuesto Especial Sobre Producción y Servicios* (IEPS), otherwise the IEPS becomes an implicit subsidy.
Source: OECD (2015), *OECD Environment Statistics* (database).

StatLink http://dx.doi.org/10.1787/888933262186

Table 2.7. **Environmentally related tax revenue**

	Revenue from environmentally related taxes						Revenue structure, %		
	% total tax revenue		% GDP		Million USD 2013	% change since 2000	Energy products	Motor vehicles and transport	Other
	2013	% points change since 2000	2013	% points change since 2000			2013	2013	2013
Australia	7.47	-0.44	2.08	-0.33	18 642	27.6	70	28	2
Austria	5.26	-0.34	2.24	-0.12	7 087	14.8	70	29	1
Belgium	4.56	-1.12	2.04	-0.45	7 650	-3.1	57	37	7
Canada	3.68	-0.12	1.13	-0.22	14 935	8.0	74	23	4
Chile	6.81	-1.56	1.38	-0.19	3 969	53.0	62	17	21
Czech Republic	8.15	0.65	2.78	0.34	7 162	56.4	77	16	7
Denmark	8.10	-1.67	3.94	-0.76	7 298	-10.1	54	39	7
Estonia	7.81	3.07	2.49	1.02	633	171.5	89	2	9
Finland	6.65	-0.02	2.91	-0.14	5 094	12.7	68	31	2
France	4.31	-0.83	1.94	-0.27	39 750	1.7	77	15	8
Germany	5.59	-0.72	2.05	-0.24	60 150	1.9	83	16	1
Greece	8.09	1.34	2.71	0.47	6 101	17.8	75	25	0
Hungary	7.09	-0.59	2.76	-0.21	4 844	15.5	73	16	11
Iceland	5.69	-2.31	2.02	-0.87	246	-2.3	64	30	7
Ireland	8.34	-0.61	2.36	-0.40	4 078	11.8	59	40	2
Israel	9.26	1.61	2.83	0.16	6 711	63.3	57	41	2
Italy	6.49	-1.12	2.78	-0.31	45 334	-10.6	77	22	1
Japan	5.37	-1.10	1.54	-0.19	62 684	-1.1	64	35	1
Korea	9.25	-2.90	2.25	-0.36	35 021	45.1	60	40	0
Luxembourg	5.65	-1.46	2.22	-0.42	811	14.1	93	7	0
Mexico	-5.81	-13.72	-0.47	-1.78	-7 466	-147.3	114	-9	-5
Netherlands	9.22	-0.40	3.44	-0.11	22 219	10.3	59	28	13
New Zealand	4.16	-0.87	1.35	-0.34	1 627	10.8	55	44	1
Norway	5.37	-1.41	2.15	-0.69	5 261	-7.7	51	46	3
Poland	6.21	0.20	1.92	-0.04	13 803	55.8	86	6	8
Portugal	6.38	-2.15	2.13	-0.48	4 773	-17.6	75	24	1
Slovak Republic	5.89	-0.84	1.74	-0.52	2 062	30.9	85	12	4
Slovenia	11.64	2.28	4.28	0.86	2 163	57.6	75	11	15
Spain	5.70	-0.86	1.86	-0.33	22 878	1.6	83	13	4
Sweden	5.51	0.06	2.36	-0.31	8 204	12.9	80	19	1
Switzerland	6.57	-0.25	1.78	-0.11	6 060	18.8	50	48	2
Turkey	13.87	2.38	4.06	1.29	42 973	147.7	71	29	0
United Kingdom	7.63	-0.59	2.51	-0.34	55 926	8.6	72	24	4
United States	3.01	-0.39	0.77	-0.20	110 623	-0.7	61	35	4
OECD	**5.16**	**-0.65**	**1.56**	**-0.26**	**629 304**	**6.2**	**69**	**27**	**3**

Note: See the Annex for country notes.
Source: OECD (2015), *OECD Environment Statistics* (database).

StatLink http://dx.doi.org/10.1787/888933262430

Environmentally related R&D

Technology development and innovation are key drivers of economic growth and productivity. They are important for managing energy and materials successfully and have a bearing on policies intended to preserve natural resources and materials and to minimise the pollution burden.

R&D budget is an input measure that indicates an economy's relative degree of investment in generating knowledge. It thus reflects current policies towards green growth.

Definitions

The indicators presented here refer to:

- Public environmentally related R&D expenditure. The data refer to government budget appropriations or outlays for R&D, expressed as a percentage of total R&D expenditure.
- Public renewable energy RD&D budgets. The data refer to government support for research, development and demonstration projects (RD&D) related to hydro, geothermal, solar, wind and other renewables. They are expressed as a percentage of total energy RD&D budgets.

Overview

Public R&D spending has increased by 20% since 2000 (in real terms); it reached a peak in 2008 and then decreased slowly to reach USD 253 billion in 2013.

Similarly, the amount dedicated to environment grew by 20.8% since 2000. After the downturn of 2008, it recovered at a faster rate than total public R&D. In 2013, it represented USD 4 billion. Its share in total, R&D remains however limited. In 2013, government R&D spending on environment represented less than 2% of total R&D in the OECD area.

But there are large differences among countries. In absolute terms, Germany, Japan and the United States are the largest funders, while New Zealand and Australia are the top investors in relative terms.

Energy related RD&D represents on average 3.7 times environmental R&D. Budgets dedicated to energy-related RD&D by OECD countries have increased by 24% since 2000, reaching USD 14.9 billion in 2013. Their share in GDP remains however very low.

The importance of renewable energy RD&D has been increasing steadily, going from 8% of total energy RD&D in 2000 to 24% in 2013. This reflects concerns about climate change, rising energy prices and the scarcity of fossil fuels.

Comparability

International comparisons should consider differences among countries in industrial structure and research capability; high R&D spending alone does not mean superior innovation performance.

For additional notes, see the Annex.

Sources

OECD (2014), "Research and Development Statistics: Government Budget Appropriations or Outlays for R&D", *OECD Science, Technology and R&D Statistics* (database), *http://dx.doi.org/10.1787/data-00194-en.*

IEA (2014), "RD&D Budget", *IEA Energy Technology RD&D Statistics* (database), *http://dx.doi.org/10.1787/data-00488-en.*

Further information

IEA, RD&D Data Online Service, *www.iea.org/statistics/RDDonlinedataservice.*

OECD (2015a), *Main Science and Technology Indicators*, Vol. 2014/2, OECD Publishing, Paris, *http://dx.doi.org/10.1787/msti-v2014-2-en.*

OECD (2015b), "Patents in environment-related technologies", *OECD Environment Statistics* (database), OECD Publishing, Paris, *http://dx.doi.org/10.1787/env-tech-pat-data-en.*

OECD (2014), "Green Growth Indicators 2014", *OECD Green Growth Studies*, OECD Publishing, Paris, *http://dx.doi.org/10.1787/9789264202030-en.*

Information on data for Israel: *http://dx.doi.org/10.1787/888932315602.*

Figure 2.18. **Environmentally related public R&D budgets, 2012-13 average**

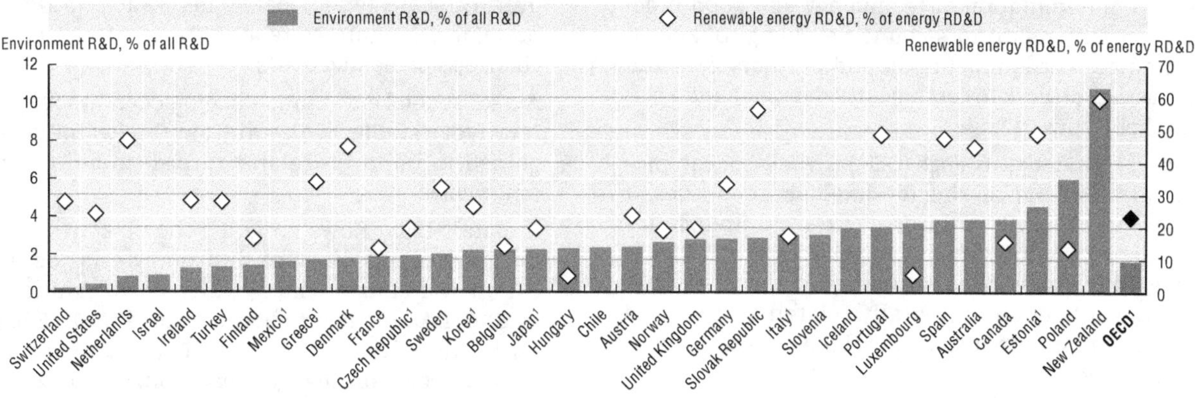

Source: IEA (2015), *IEA Energy Technology RD&D Statistics* (database); OECD (2015), *OECD Science, Technology and R&D Statistics* (database).

StatLink http://dx.doi.org/10.1787/888933262198

Table 2.8. **Environmentally related public R&D budgets**

	Environment R&D		Total R&D			Renewable energy RD&D		Energy RD&D		
	% total R&D		% GDP	Million USD	% change since 2000-01	% energy RD&D		% GDP	Million USD	% change since 2000-01
	2012-13 average	% points change since 2000-01	2012-13 average	2012-13 average		2012-13 average	% points change since 2000-01	2012-13 average	2012-13 average	
Australia	3.9	0.9	0.4	3 948	16.7	44.7	34.8	0.06	493	279
Austria	2.4	0.9	0.8	2 495	52.0	23.5	-3.7	0.04	120	270
Belgium	2.2	-0.7	0.6	2 401	34.0	14.0	0.0	0.03	121	..
Canada	3.9	-0.6	0.5	6 841	21.6	15.5	5.6	0.07	908	250
Chile	2.3	..	0.2	644	..	..	..	..	..	..
Czech Republic	1.9	-1.5	0.7	1 690	79.0	19.4	9.6	0.02	52	302
Denmark	1.8	-0.8	1.0	1 889	48.2	44.7	5.1	0.06	107	154
Estonia	4.5	-1.5	0.8	208	297.5	48.7	..	0.05	14	..
Finland	1.4	-0.8	1.0	1 788	26.4	16.3	3.0	0.12	206	201
France	1.9	-0.4	0.7	14 659	-13.2	13.4	10.4	0.05	1 078	78
Germany	2.8	-0.4	0.9	26 066	31.6	33.2	7.6	0.03	828	144
Greece	1.7	-2.8	0.4	971	44.9	33.8	-1.2	0.00	8	-25
Hungary	2.3	..	0.5	874	0.0	4.8	-22.7	0.09	153	2 535
Iceland	3.4	2.8	1.0	124	52.8	..	..	..	..	..
Ireland	1.2	0.9	0.4	742	85.6	28.0	12.9	0.02	36	746
Israel	0.9	-0.2	0.6	1 471	14.6	..	..	..	..	..
Italy	3.0	0.8	0.5	8 794	-16.2	17.3	6.3	0.02	406	14
Japan	2.2	1.4	0.8	30 869	26.4	19.6	15.6	0.07	2 799	-11
Korea	2.2	-2.0	1.0	14 475	146.1	26.2	15.2	0.04	669	345
Luxembourg	3.7	0.8	0.7	240	632.7	5.4	..	0.16	58	..
Mexico	1.6	0.5	0.2	3 784	49.8	..	..	..	..	..
Netherlands	0.8	-2.5	0.7	4 756	9.7	46.5	21.5	0.03	199	12
New Zealand	10.8	0.0	0.5	586	25.2	59.3	22.5	0.01	11	109
Norway	2.6	-0.1	0.8	1 924	44.3	18.8	8.5	0.10	237	376
Poland	6.0	5.9	0.4	2 561	46.9	13.5	..	0.03	196	..
Portugal	3.5	-0.6	0.9	2 073	63.9	48.6	1.0	0.00	3	59
Slovak Republic	2.9	1.3	0.4	470	93.8	56.1	..	0.02	20	..
Slovenia	3.0	1.0	0.5	256	28.0	..	..	..	..	..
Spain	3.8	0.0	0.6	6 995	7.9	47.4	15.4	0.02	192	149
Sweden	2.0	0.9	0.8	2 903	47.2	32.1	-0.3	0.03	117	47
Switzerland	0.2	0.0	0.9	2 917	83.3	27.7	4.6	0.04	122	22
Turkey	1.3	..	0.3	3 588	..	27.8	4.9	0.00	11	29
United Kingdom	2.8	0.7	0.6	12 269	4.1	19.2	5.8	0.02	445	548
United States	0.4	-0.2	0.8	119 950	23.4	24.1	15.0	0.04	5 323	89
OECD	**1.6**	**0.0**	**0.7**	**286 222**	**25.9**	**23.1**	**14.3**	**0.04**	**14 931**	**75**

Note: See the Annex for country notes.

Source: IEA (2015), *IEA Energy Technology RD&D Statistics* (database); OECD (2015), *OECD Science, Technology and R&D Statistics* (database).

StatLink http://dx.doi.org/10.1787/888933262448

Environmentally related ODA

International financial flows have an important role in the uptake and dissemination of technology and good practices. They contribute to cross-country exchange of knowledge, stimulate entrepreneurship and partnerships, and are a key aspect of work to combine development and environmental objectives.

Official development assistance (ODA) is vital as it can provide crucial funds and backing for developing countries. It makes up more than two thirds of external finance for least-developed countries. About two-thirds of total ODA is channelled directly by donors to partner countries. ODA directed towards environmentally related sectors and objectives is an important source of financing for sustainable development.

Definitions

The indicators presented here refer to bilateral ODA allocated to environmentally related sectors. The data refer to gross disbursements allocated to general environmental protection, water supply and sanitation, and renewable energy. They are expressed as a percentage of total sector-allocable ODA.

Information on net ODA (i.e. net disbursements of bilateral ODA) expressed as a percentage of Gross National Income (GNI) is given as a complement.

Overview

Aid to developing countries has increased by 66% in real terms since 2000. It reached a first peak in 2010, then fell in 2011-12 as many governments took austerity measures and trimmed aid budgets. In 2013, net aid provided by members of the OECD Development Assistance Committee (DAC) rose by 6.1% in real terms to reach the highest level ever recorded (USD 134.8 billion), despite continued pressure on budgets in OECD countries. Five DAC member countries exceed the United Nations target of keeping ODA at 0.7% of GNI, but the collective effort of DAC members fell short of the target (i.e. at 0.3%).

Environmental sustainability is increasingly being mainstreamed in development co-operation, and aid targeted at environmentally related sectors and objectives has been gaining from the increased availability of aid resources. In 2013, gross disbursements amounted to USD 9.5 billion, a 244% increase since 2002 in real terms. Its share in total ODA increased from 9.6% to 12.6% over the same period, mainly thanks to stronger support for programmes related to water and climate change as of the mid-2000s.

Aid for general environmental protection has remained relatively stable, while aid for renewable energy gained in importance and surpassed aid for non-renewables.

In parallel, aid flows targeting the objectives of the Rio Conventions, i.e. related to biodiversity, desertification and climate change, increased significantly. In 2013, DAC members allocated some USD 5.8 billion for biodiversity related aid, USD 15.2 billion for aid related to climate change mitigation, USD 10.2 billion for aid related to climate change adaptation, and USD 2.8 billion for desertification related aid.

Comparability

Data on ODA are standardised through the OECD Development Assistance Committee (DAC) Creditor Reporting System (CRS). ODA donors are requested to screen each aid activity reported to the CRS, but data gaps remain for some donors, and it remains difficult to determine the environmental purpose of existing aid commitments and investment projects.

Latest available year: data prior to 2010 were not considered.

For additional notes, see the Annex.

Sources

OECD (2014), "Creditor Reporting System: Aid activities", *OECD International Development Statistics* (database), *http://dx.doi.org/10.1787/data-00061-en*.

Further information

OECD (2014), "Green Growth Indicators 2014", *OECD Green Growth Studies*, OECD Publishing, Paris, *http://dx.doi.org/10.1787/9789264202030-en*.

OECD (2014), *Development Co-Operation Report 2014: Mobilising Resources for Sustainable Development*, OECD Publishing, Paris, *http://dx.doi.org/10.1787/dcr-2014-en*.

Information on data for Israel: *http://dx.doi.org/10.1787/888932315602*.

Figure 2.19. **Official Development Assistance (ODA) for environment and renewable energy, 2013**

Gross disbursements as percentage of total ODA

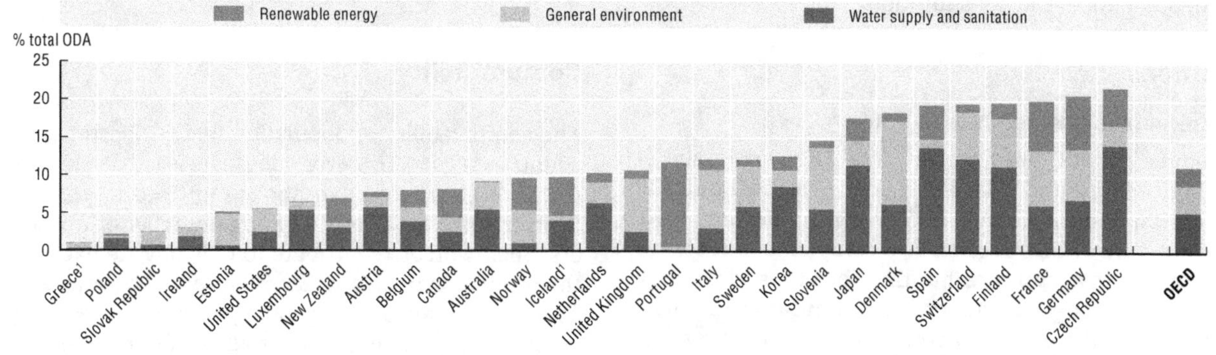

Source: OECD (2014), "Creditor Reporting System: Aid Activities", *OECD International Development Statistics* (database), *http://dx.doi.org/10.1787/data-00061-en.*

StatLink http://dx.doi.org/10.1787/888933262201

Table 2.9. **Official Development Assistance (ODA) for environment and renewable energy**

	Water supply and sanitation		Renewable energy		General environment		Net ODA	
	% sector-allocable ODA		% sector-allocable ODA		% sector-allocable ODA		% GNI	
	2013 or latest	% points change since 2002	2013 or latest	% points change since 2002	2013 or latest	% points change since 2002	2013	% points change since 2000
Australia	5.41	1.96	0.05	-0.05	3.65	1.13	0.33	0.06
Austria	5.68	1.00	0.58	0.08	1.44	-1.31	0.27	0.04
Belgium	3.79	1.28	2.24	2.23	1.92	0.64	0.45	0.09
Canada	2.43	-0.40	3.71	2.78	1.96	-3.11	0.27	0.02
Chile	..	..	..	..	..	..	..	..
Czech Republic	14.13	..	4.84	..	2.72	..	0.11	0.08
Denmark	6.32	-3.57	1.10	0.46	11.02	2.85	0.85	-0.21
Estonia	0.56	..	0.24	..	4.27	..	0.13	0.12
Finland	11.31	3.30	2.02	2.05	6.43	1.69	0.54	0.23
France	6.18	0.73	6.45	6.04	7.40	1.17	0.41	0.11
Germany	6.95	-2.88	7.06	2.68	6.75	4.96	0.38	0.11
Greece	0.28	-0.67	0.04	..	0.64	-4.33	0.10	-0.10
Hungary	..	..	..	..	..	..	0.10	0.07
Iceland	3.95	..	5.09	..	0.71	..	0.25	0.15
Ireland	1.75	-5.70	0.01	-0.02	1.19	0.69	0.46	0.17
Israel	..	..	..	..	..	..	0.07	-0.07
Italy	3.02	1.80	1.31	1.19	7.76	-7.05	0.17	0.04
Japan	11.44	0.61	2.87	1.88	3.34	1.78	0.23	-0.05
Korea	8.56	..	1.79	..	2.23	..	0.13	0.09
Luxembourg	5.31	..	0.10	..	1.02	..	1.00	0.30
Mexico	..	..	..	..	..	..	..	..
Netherlands	6.30	0.36	1.22	0.95	2.77	-4.43	0.67	-0.17
New Zealand	3.00	1.69	3.21	2.61	0.62	0.35	0.26	0.01
Norway	1.02	-2.20	4.19	3.39	4.40	-0.12	1.07	0.31
Poland	1.55	..	0.28	..	0.31	..	0.10	0.08
Portugal	0.14	-0.13	11.10	10.56	0.48	-0.09	0.23	-0.03
Slovak Republic	0.70	..	0.05	..	1.71	..	0.09	0.06
Slovenia	5.63	..	0.91	..	8.16	..	0.13	..
Spain	13.79	10.43	4.43	4.11	1.23	-1.61	0.17	-0.05
Sweden	5.92	-0.03	0.89	0.66	5.33	1.32	1.01	0.21
Switzerland	12.33	5.85	1.02	-0.02	6.26	-3.17	0.47	0.15
Turkey	..	..	..	..	..	..	0.42	0.38
United Kingdom	2.56	-0.53	1.02	0.91	7.05	5.74	0.71	0.39
United States	2.42	0.20	0.06	-0.06	3.05	-0.40	0.18	0.08
OECD average	**5.26**	**0.54**	**2.34**	**1.74**	**3.65**	**-0.54**	**0.37**	**0.08**

Note: See the Annex for country notes.

Source: OECD (2014), "Creditor Reporting System: Aid activities", *OECD International Development Statistics* (database), http://dx.doi.org/10.1787/data-00061-en.

StatLink http://dx.doi.org/10.1787/888933262453

GDP, population and consumption

This section provides important socio-economic background information, particularly with regard to economic growth, population and consumption.

Definitions

The indicators presented here refer to:

- Economic growth. They present total GDP, expressed at 2005 price levels and purchasing power parities, and GDP per capita, and the change in GDP per capita since 1990. The structure of GDP is given as a complement. It shows value added in agriculture (hunting, forestry and fishing); industry (mining and quarrying, manufacturing, gas, electricity and water, and construction); and services. Value added excludes financial intermediation services indirectly measured.
- Population growth and density. They present changes in national resident population (all nationals present in or temporarily absent from a country, and aliens permanently settled in the country), as well as population densities (the number of residents compared to the total area of the country) and an "ageing index" (the ratios between the population over 64 and under 15).
- Private consumption, i.e. by households and private non-profit institutions serving households. They present private final consumption expenditure expressed as % of GDP and per capita, as well as the structure of private consumption. Private final consumption expenditure is the largest component of final uses of GDP, representing in general around 70% of GDP. It represents the sum of: i) the outlays of resident households on new durable and non-durable goods and services less their net sales of second-hand goods, scraps and wastes; and ii) the value of goods and services produced by private non-profit institutions for own use on current account. It is expressed at 2005 price levels and purchasing power parities. Rent refers to imputed rent.
- Government consumption, presenting general government final consumption expenditure expressed as percentage of GDP and per capita. Total general government final consumption is important as a component of total GDP, and reflects the government's direct role as a "consumer" of final goods and services. It represents the value of goods and services produced by governments for their own use on current account; and is expressed at 2005 price levels and purchasing power parities.

Comparability

The comparability of population and GDP estimates across countries is good. However, some care is needed in interpretation, for example Luxembourg and, to a lesser extent, Switzerland have a relatively large number of frontier workers. Such workers contribute to GDP but are excluded from the population figures, which is one of the reasons why cross-country comparisons of income per capita based on gross or net national income (GDI and NNI) are often preferred.

The comparability of private consumption expenditure is good, that of general government expenditure is high.

For additional notes, see the Annex.

Sources

OECD (2015), "Aggregate National Accounts: Gross Domestic Product", *OECD National Accounts Statistics* (database), *http://dx.doi.org/10.1787/na-ana-data-en*.

OECD (2014), "OECD Economic Outlook No. 95", *OECD Economic Outlook: Statistics and Projections* (database), *http://dx.doi.org/10.1787/eo-data-en*.

OECD (2014), "Population projections", *OECD Historical Population Data and Projections Statistics* (database), *http://dx.doi.org/10.1787/lfs-lfs-data-en*.

FAO (2015), FAOSTAT (database), *http://faostat3.fao.org*.

World Bank (2015), *World Bank Open Data*, *http://data.worldbank.org*.

Further information

OECD (2014), *National Accounts at a Glance 2014*, OECD Publishing, Paris, *http://dx.doi.org/10.1787/na_glance-2014-en*.

Information on data for Israel: *http://dx.doi.org/10.1787/888932315602*.

Figure 2.20. **Gross Domestic Product (GDP) per capita, 2013**

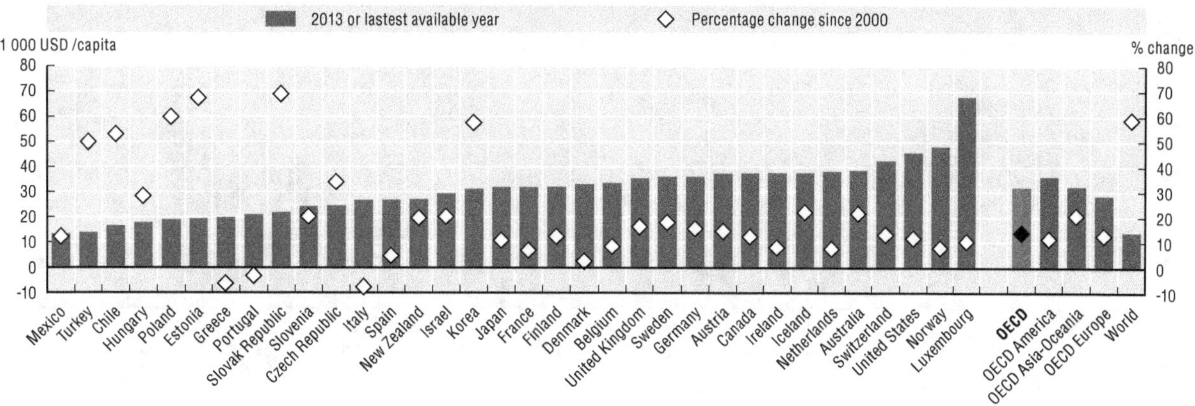

Source: OECD (2015), *Historical Population Data and Projections* (database); OECD (2015), *OECD National Accounts Statistics* (database); World Bank (2015), *World Bank Open Data.*

StatLink http://dx.doi.org/10.1787/888933262216

Table 2.10. **Gross Domestic Product (GDP)**

	Gross domestic product				Structure of value added		
	Total	Per capita			Agriculture	Industry	Services
	Billion USD	1 000 USD	% change	% change		%	
	2013	2013	1990-2013	2000-13	2013	2013	2013
Australia	895	38.7	54.2	21.4	2.4	26.8	70.7
Austria	317	37.4	42.1	14.4	1.4	28.2	70.3
Belgium	376	33.6	31.7	8.4	0.8	22.5	76.7
Canada	1 325	37.5	34.4	12.3	1.5	27.7	70.8
Chile	288	16.4	148.7	53.0	3.4	35.3	61.3
Czech Republic	258	24.5	42.1	34.1	2.6	36.7	60.7
Denmark	185	33.2	28.5	2.5	1.4	22.9	75.8
Estonia	25	19.3	77.9	67.3	3.6	28.9	67.5
Finland	175	32.1	35.6	12.3	2.7	26.9	70.5
France	2 048	32.0	26.2	6.8	1.7	19.8	78.5
Germany	2 933	36.2	35.6	15.5	0.9	30.7	68.4
Greece	225	19.8	11.2	-6.3	3.8	13.8	82.4
Hungary	176	17.8	33.0	28.3	4.4	30.2	65.4
Iceland	12	37.7	43.1	22.0	7.7	24.5	67.8
Ireland	173	37.7	98.4	8.0	1.6	24.1	74.3
Israel	237	29.4	59.6	20.2	..	..	..
Italy	1 628	26.6	8.3	-7.7	2.3	23.3	74.4
Japan	4 071	32.0	20.6	10.7	1.2	25.6	73.2
Korea	1 558	31.0	170.5	57.6	2.3	38.6	59.1
Luxembourg	36	67.9	58.0	10.4	0.3	12.2	87.5
Mexico	1 588	13.4	36.3	12.3	3.5	34.8	61.7
Netherlands	647	38.4	38.0	7.5	2.0	22.2	75.9
New Zealand	121	27.0	42.6	19.6	7.2	23.8	69.1
Norway	245	48.2	46.2	7.9	1.5	40.8	57.7
Poland	719	18.9	128.6	59.8	3.3	33.2	63.5
Portugal	224	20.9	24.7	-3.3	2.3	21.1	76.7
Slovak Republic	118	21.8	77.4	68.9	4.0	33.2	62.7
Slovenia	50	24.2	44.6	20.2	2.1	32.0	65.8
Spain	1 233	26.8	33.0	4.7	2.8	23.3	73.9
Sweden	348	36.2	40.5	17.9	1.4	25.9	72.7
Switzerland	341	42.5	19.0	13.0	0.7	25.7	73.6
Turkey	1 057	13.9	78.8	49.8	8.5	27.1	64.4
United Kingdom	2 228	35.6	43.1	16.2	0.7	20.2	79.2
United States	14 452	45.7	38.5	11.6	1.3	21.0	77.7
OECD	**40 311**	**32.1**	**38.2**	**13.8**	**1.4**	**23.8**	**74.7**
OECD America	17 653	36.2	37.4	11.4	..	..	..
OECD Asia-Oceania	6 881	32.3	42.3	20.6	..	..	..
OECD Europe	15 777	28.4	34.9	12.6	..	..	..
World	99 447	14.0	58.7	37.0	..	..	..

Source: OECD (2015), *OECD Historical Population Data and Projections* (database); OECD (2015), OECD National Accounts Statistics (database); World Bank (2015), *World Bank Open Data.*

StatLink http://dx.doi.org/10.1787/888933262461

Figure 2.21. **Population density, 2013**

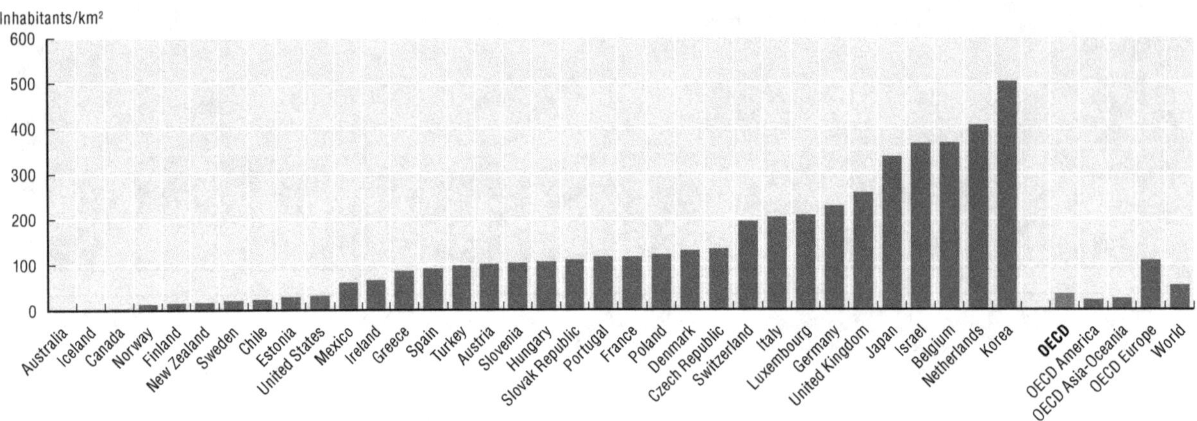

Source: OECD (2015), *OECD Historical Population Data and Projections Statistics* (database); FAO (2015), FAOSTAT (database).

StatLink http://dx.doi.org/10.1787/888933262221

Table 2.11. **Population density and ageing**

	Total	Change	Change	Density	Ageing index		
	1 000 inhabitants	%	%	Inh./km²	Pop. > 64/pop. < 15		
	2013	1990-2013	2000-13	2013	1990	2000	2013
Australia	23 132	36	22	3	50	60	76
Austria	8 469	10	6	101	85	91	127
Belgium	11 196	12	9	367	82	95	104
Canada	35 317	28	15	4	55	65	93
Chile	17 557	33	14	23	20	26	46
Czech Republic	10 520	2	2	133	58	84	115
Denmark	5 582	9	5	130	91	80	102
Estonia	1 320	-16	-4	29	52	85	115
Finland	5 440	9	5	16	69	82	116
France	64 046	13	8	117	70	85	99
Germany	81 059	2	-1	227	93	105	163
Greece	11 361	12	4	86	71	109	139
Hungary	9 887	-5	-3	106	66	90	120
Iceland	322	26	15	3	43	50	62
Ireland	4 593	31	21	65	42	51	56
Israel	8 057	73	28	365	29	34	38
Italy	61 178	8	7	203	90	128	149
Japan	127 296	3	0	337	66	119	195
Korea	50 220	17	7	501	20	34	83
Luxembourg	537	41	23	207	77	74	87
Mexico	118 395	36	17	60	11	15	23
Netherlands	16 851	13	6	406	70	73	100
New Zealand	4 472	32	16	17	49	52	71
Norway	5 080	20	13	13	86	76	86
Poland	38 056	0	-1	122	41	63	97
Portugal	10 723	7	4	116	66	99	125
Slovak Republic	5 416	2	1	110	41	59	88
Slovenia	2 085	4	5	103	52	88	117
Spain	46 046	19	14	91	69	114	116
Sweden	9 610	12	8	21	99	94	121
Switzerland	8 018	19	12	194	85	88	128
Turkey	76 055	36	13	97	13	23	31
United Kingdom	62 571	9	6	257	83	83	97
United States	316 129	27	12	32	58	58	73
OECD	**1 256 596**	**18**	**9**	**35**	**52**	**64**	**86**
OECD America	487 398	29	14	22	40	43	57
OECD Asia-Oceania	213 176	11	5	25	50	82	137
OECD Europe	556 022	11	6	108	63	79	100
World	7 162 120	35	17	53	..	..	..

Note: See the Annex for country notes.
Source: OECD (2015), *OECD Historical Population Data and Projections Statistics* (database); FAO (2015), FAOSTAT (database).

StatLink http://dx.doi.org/10.1787/888933262478

Figure 2.22. **Private and government final consumption expenditure, 2013 or latest available year**

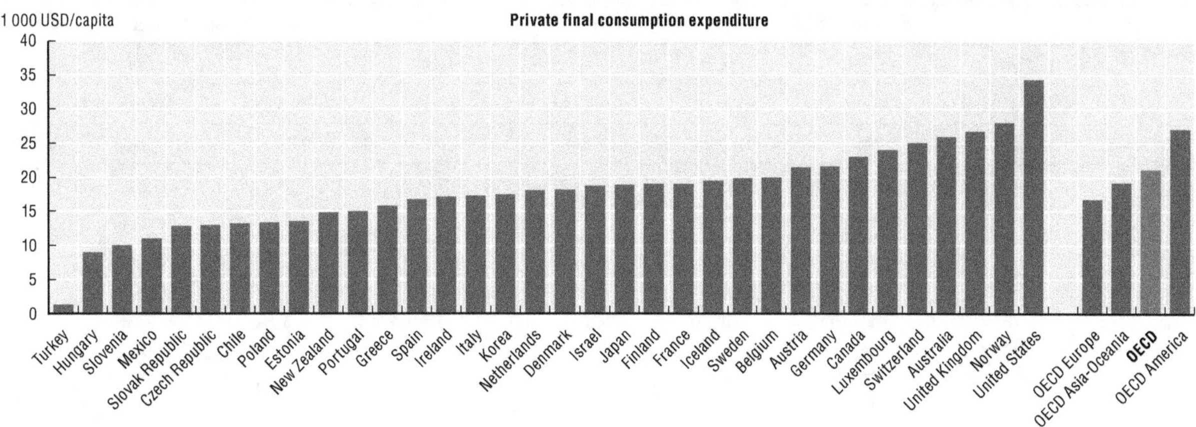

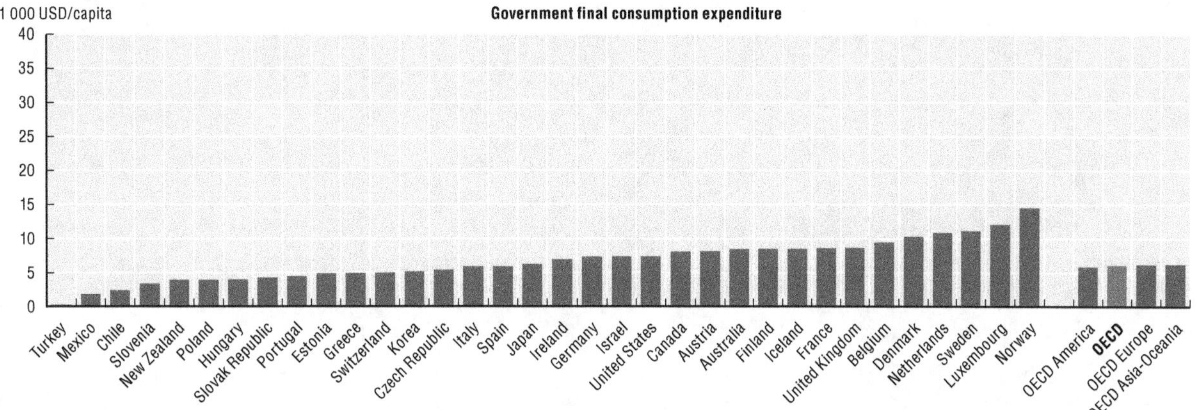

Source: OECD (2014), "OECD Economic Outlook No. 95", *OECD Economic Outlook: Statistics and Projections* (database), OECD (2015), *OECD Historical Population Data and Projections Statistics* (database).

StatLink http://dx.doi.org/10.1787/888933262236

Figure 2.23. **Private final consumption expenditure by type, 2013 or latest available year**

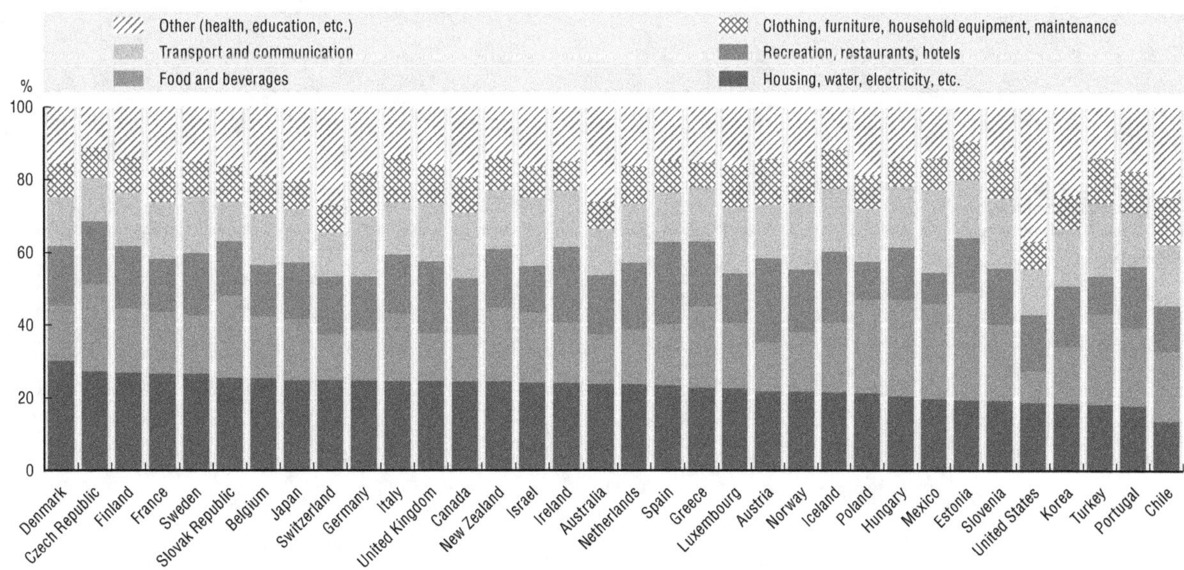

Source: OECD (2015), *OECD National Accounts Statistics* (database).

StatLink http://dx.doi.org/10.1787/888933262246

Table 2.12. **Private and government final consumption expenditure**

	Private final consumption expenditure				Government final consumption expenditure			
	Total	Per capita			Total	Per capita		
	% GDP	1 000 USD	% change	% change	% GDP	1 000 USD	% change	% change
	2013	2013	1990-2013	2000-13	2013	2013	1990-2013	2000-13
Australia	54	26	58	27	17	8	44	21
Austria	54	21	30	10	20	8	40	13
Belgium	51	20	22	6	24	9	28	11
Canada	56	23	48	27	21	8	12	17
Chile	64	13	124	88	13	2	70	55
Czech Republic	48	13	51	29	19	5	27	21
Denmark	49	18	29	11	27	10	38	14
Estonia	52	13	166	77	19	5	49	51
Finland	55	19	39	25	25	8	16	11
France	55	19	28	10	24	9	30	15
Germany	55	22	27	12	19	7	40	19
Greece	71	16	12	-3	19	5	15	1
Hungary	51	9	43	23	19	4	21	27
Iceland	53	19	34	6	24	8	33	13
Ireland	46	17	76	9	16	7	59	13
Israel	56	19	42	23	23	7	7	5
Italy	61	17	7	-9	19	6	1	-2
Japan	60	19	26	13	20	6	63	23
Korea	50	17	128	42	15	5	136	73
Luxembourg	31	24	27	4	18	12	67	26
Mexico	68	11	46	23	12	2	8	5
Netherlands	45	18	24	-4	26	11	52	32
New Zealand	57	15	56	36	18	4	32	26
Norway	41	28	87	42	22	14	59	26
Poland	60	13	155	55	18	4	102	44
Portugal	65	15	31	-2	19	4	35	0
Slovak Republic	57	13	105	54	18	4	55	48
Slovenia	53	10	..	14	19	3	..	18
Spain	59	17	25	1	19	6	70	30
Sweden	47	20	38	22	26	11	14	7
Switzerland	53	25	16	9	11	5	9	5
Turkey	70	1	76	47	15	0	103	54
United Kingdom	64	27	57	17	20	9	37	22
United States	67	34	51	18	15	7	2	4
OECD	**65**	**21**	**..**	**17**	**19**	**6**	**..**	**14**
OECD America	73	27	..	19	16	6	..	5
OECD Asia-Oceania	58	19	..	21	19	6	..	30
OECD Europe	58	17	..	10	22	6	..	17

Note: See the Annex for country notes.

Source: OECD (2014), "OECD Economic Outlook No. 95", *OECD Economic Outlook: Statistics and Projections* (database), OECD (2015), *OECD Historical Population Data and Projections Statistics* (database).

StatLink http://dx.doi.org/10.1787/888933262481

ANNEX

Additional information and country notes

Greenhouse gas (GHG) emissions

The main international agreement is the United Nations Framework Convention on Climate Change (Rio de Janeiro, 1992), ratified by 196 parties. Industrialised countries committed to taking measures aimed at stabilising GHG emissions by 2000 at 1990 levels. The 1997 Kyoto Protocol established differentiated national or regional emission reduction or limitation targets for the six major GHGs (CO_2, CH_4, N_2O, PFCs, HFCs and SF_6) for 2008-12, with 1990 as the reference year. The Kyoto Protocol has been ratified by 192 countries, including all but two OECD countries, and has been in force since 16 February 2005. In 2010 and 2011, negotiations in Copenhagen and Cancun led to progress on, among other things, goals for emission reductions, including from developing countries; finance; adaptation; and reducing emissions from deforestation and degradation (REDD).

Data presented in this report refer to the sum of all six "Kyoto gases" expressed in CO_2 equivalents (status of the UNFCCC and the Kyoto Protocol: as of May 2014). They do however not directly relate to the Kyoto targets; they refer to domestic emissions (i.e. emitted within the national territory) and exclude CO_2 emissions and removals from land use, land-use change and forestry; they do not take account of international transactions of emission reduction units or certified emission reductions.

- Latest available year: data prior to 2009 were not considered.

Israel and Korea. Latest available year: 2011.

Mexico. Latest available year: 2010. Data include emissions or removals from land-use change and forestry (LUCF)

OECD and OECD Asia-Oceania. Do not include Israel.

SO_X and NO_X emissions

An important international agreement for Europe and North America is the Convention on Long-Range Transboundary Air Pollution (Geneva, 1979), and its protocols to reduce emissions of sulphur (Helsinki, 1985; Oslo, 1994; Gothenburg, 1999), and nitrogen oxides (Sofia, 1988; Gothenburg, 1999). Other protocols aim at reducing emissions of VOCs (Geneva, 1991; Gothenburg, 1999), ammonia (Gothenburg, 1999), heavy metals (Aarhus, 1998) and persistent organic pollutants (Aarhus, 1998). In 2012, the Gothenburg Protocol was revised to set more ambitious targets to reduce emissions by 2020 and beyond, including targets for fine particulate matter (among which is black carbon, a climate-forcing pollutant).

- Data refer to man-made emissions only. SO_X and NO_X are given as quantities of SO_2 and NO_2 respectively. Emissions from international transport (aviation, marine) are excluded.

- Data may include provisional figures and Secretariat estimates. For some countries expert estimates from EMEP have been used: Czech Republic forthe year 2012; Poland for the year 1990.
- Percentage change: change with respect to the latest available year since 1990. Latest available year: data prior to 2009 were not considered.

Australia. NO_X: excludes prescribed burning of savannas (681 000 tonnes in 2012).

Iceland. SO_X: includes H_2S emissions from geothermal power plants (expressed as SO_2; these emissions represented 68 000 tonnes in 2012, i.e. 80% of total emissions).

Israel and Korea. Latest available year: 2011.

Luxembourg. Data exclude "fuel tourism" emissions (resulting from lower taxation of road fuels compared to neighbouring countries).

New Zealand. NO_X: excludes prescribed burning of savannas.

OECD. Secretariat estimates, do not include Chile and Mexico.

Table A.1. **Emission ceilings relating to the provision of Article 3, paragraphs 1 and 10 of the Gothenburg Protocol**[a]

	Sulphur emissions (1 000 tonnes of SO_2 per year)				Protocol status[b]	Nitrogen oxide emissions (1 000 tonnes of NO_2 per year)			
	Levels 1980	Levels 1990	Ceilings for 2010	% reductions for2010 (base year 1990)		Levels 1990	Ceilings for 2010	% reductions for 2010 (base year 1990)	
Austria	400	91	39	-57	S	194	107	-45	Austria
Belgium	828	372	106	-72	R	339	181	-47	Belgium
Canada national	4 643	3 236	..	..	S	2 104	..	..	Canada
Canada PEMA[c]	3 135	1 873	..	..					
Czech Republic	2 257	1 876	283	-85	R	742	286	-61	Czech Republic
Denmark	450	182	55	-70	R	282	127	-55	Denmark
Finland	584	260	116	-55	R	300	170	-43	Finland
France	3 208	1 269	400	-68	R	1 882	860	-54	France
Germany	7 514	5 313	550	-90	R	2 693	1 081	-60	Germany
Greece	400	509	546	7	S	343	344	0	Greece
Hungary	1 633	1 010	550	-46	R	238	198	-17	Hungary
Ireland	222	178	42	-76	S	115	65	-43	Ireland
Italy	3 757	1 651	500	-70	S	1 938	1 000	-48	Italy
Luxembourg	24	15	4	-73	R	23	11	-52	Luxembourg
Netherlands	490	202	50	-75	R	580	266	-54	Netherlands
Norway	137	53	22	-58	R	218	156	-28	Norway
Poland	4 100	3 210	1 397	-56	S	1 280	879	-31	Poland
Portugal	266	362	170	-53	R	348	260	-25	Portugal
Slovak Republic	780	543	110	-80	R	225	130	-42	Slovak Republic
Slovenia	234	196	27	-86	R	63	45	-29	Slovenia
Spain	2 959	2 182	774	-65	R	1 113	847	-24	Spain*
Sweden	491	119	67	-44	R	338	148	-56	Sweden
Switzerland	116	43	26	-40	R	166	79	-52	Switzerland
United Kingdom	4 863	3 731	625	-83	R	2 673	1 181	-56	United Kingdom
USA	..	..	..	..	R	..	..	..	USA
European Community	26 456	16 436	4 059	-75	R	13 161	6 671	-49	European Community

a) 1980 and 1990 emission levels and the % reductions listed are given for information purposes only in the Annex II of the Gothenburg protocol. See the protocol text for details and country notes (*www.unece.org/env/lrtap*).

b) As of 24 May 2012, the date of entry into force of the protocol. S: signed, R: ratified. N.B. In 1991 Canada and the United States signed a bilateral air quality agreement including an acid rain (1991) and an ozone annex (2000).

c) PEMA: pollutant emission management areas. The PEMA for sulphur for Canada is an area of 1 million square kilometres which includes all the territory of the Provinces of Prince Edward Island, Nova Scotia and New Brunswick, all the territory of the Province of Québec south of a straight line between Havre-St. Pierre on the north coast of the Gulf of Saint Lawrence and the point where the Québec-Ontario boundary intersects with the James Bay coastline, and all the territory of the Province of Ontario south of a straight line between the point where the Ontario-Québec boundary intersects the James Bay coastline and the Nipigon River near the north shore of Lake Superior.

Particulate emissions and population exposure

Emissions of fine particulates

The main international agreement is the Protocol to Abate Acidification, Eutrophication and Ground-level Ozone (Gothenburg Protocol) under the UNECE Convention on Long-Range Transboundary Air Pollution (Air Convention). This protocol, signed in 1999 and revised in 2012, includes national emission reductions targets for $PM_{2.5}$ to be achieved by 2020.

- The data presented refer to man-made emissions of fine particulates smaller than 2.5 microns.

Population exposure to fine particulates

The data presented in the report refer to population weighted concentrations of fine particulates and to the population exposed to concentration levels above WHO guideline values. They should be considered as a general indication of air quality, intended for cross-country comparisons of the relative risk of particulate matter pollution. Actual concentrations and exposure levels may differ, as pollutant concentrations are very sensitive to local conditions, and measurement methods are not the same for all countries.

- Population-weighted exposure to ambient $PM_{2.5}$ pollution is defined as the average level of exposure of a nation's population to outdoor concentrations of suspended particulates measuring less than 2.5 microns in diameter. Exposure is calculated by weighting mean annual concentrations of $PM_{2.5}$ by population in both urban and rural areas and by aggregating them at the national level. Estimates of annual concentrations of very fine particulates are produced by the *Global Burden of Diseases, Injuries, and Risk Factors Study* (GBD), an international scientific effort led by the Institute for Health Metrics and Evaluation at the University of Washington (*http://www.healthdata.org/gbd/about*). They are generated by combining data from atmospheric chemistry transport models, satellite observations of aerosols in the atmosphere, and ground-level monitoring of particulates. More details can be found in the van Donkelaar et al. 2015 article, "Use of Satellite Observations for Long-Term Exposure Assessment of Global Concentrations of Fine Particulate Matter", in the journal *Environmental Health Perspectives*, 123:135-143; *http://dx.doi.org/10.1289/chp.1408646*.

  See also: Mean annual exposure to $PM_{2.5}$ (microgrammes per cubic meter): *http://data.worldbank.org/indicator/EN.ATM.PM25.MC.M3*.

- The population exposed to ambient concentrations of $PM_{2.5}$ that exceed the WHO guideline value is defined as the portion of a country's population living in places where mean annual concentrations of $PM_{2.5}$ are greater than 10 microgrammes per cubic meter. The data are obtained by overlaying $PM_{2.5}$ concentration estimates with gridded population data. The per cent of inhabitants that live in areas where $PM_{2.5}$ concentrations exceed recommended levels is calculated by summing the population for grid cells where $PM_{2.5}$ concentrations are beyond a threshold value, and then dividing by total population.

  See also: Population exposed to $PM_{2.5}$ levels exceeding the WHO guideline value (% of total): *http://data.worldbank.org/indicator/EN.ATM.PM25.MC.ZS*.

- 10 microgrammes per cubic meter is the long-term guideline value recommended by the World Health Organization (WHO) as the lower end of the range of concentrations over which adverse health effects due to $PM_{2.5}$ exposure have been observed. The value recommended in the European Union is a three-year running annual average exposure concentration inferior to 20 $\mu g/m^3$ (legally binding in 2015). It is based on averages over selected monitoring stations in agglomerations and larger urban areas set in urban background locations to best assess the $PM_{2.5}$ exposure to the general population: *http://ec.europa.eu/environment/air/quality/standards.htm*.

Freshwater abstraction and intensity of use

The intensity of use of natural freshwater resources (or water stress) is expressed as gross abstraction in % of total available renewable freshwater resources (including inflows from neighbouring countries) or in % of internal freshwater resources (i.e. precipitation – evapotranspiration). The following stress levels can be distinguished:

- Low (less than 10%): generally there is no major stress on the available resources.
- Moderate (10% to 20%): indicates that water availability issues are becoming a constraint on development and significant investments are needed to provide adequate supplies.
- Medium-high (20% to 40%): implies the management of both supply and demand, and conflicts among competing uses need to be resolved.
- High (more than 40%): indicates serious scarcity, and usually shows unsustainable water use, which can become a limiting factor in social and economic development.

National water stress levels may hide important variations at subnational (e.g. river basin) level, in particular in countries with extensive arid and semi-arid regions.

- For some countries the data refer to water permits (e.g. Chile, Mexico, New Zealand) and not to actual abstractions.
- Freshwater resources: the data refer to long-term annual averages over a minimum period of 30 consecutive years.
- Latest year available: data prior to 2009 were not considered.
- Data on irrigated areas refer to the area equipped for irrigation. *Source:* FAO.

Austria. Data for freshwater abstractions as a % of resources represent a 1981-2010 long-term average.

Belgium. Freshwater resources: do not include underground flows and include estimates.

Czech Republic. Freshwater resources: do not include underground flows. Total abstractions decreased in 2013 due to lower water abstraction for cooling in electricity production.

Denmark. Irrigation includes abstractions for fish farming.

France. Data refer to metropolitan France and to overseas departments.

Germany. Freshwater abstractions: totals up to 1998 do not include agricultural uses other than irrigation.

Ireland. Break in series in 2005 (change in methodology).

Japan. Public supply: data refer to abstractions supplied to households and the service sector only.

Mexico. From 2001: volumes of water granted in concessions; prior data are estimates.

New Zealand. Data exclude abstractions from storage water. Estimates based on water permits, assuming that actual abstractions are equal to 50% of water allocations.

Poland. Abstractions for agriculture include aquaculture (areas over 10 ha) and irrigation (arable land and forest areas greater than 20 ha). Water for animal production and domestic needs of rural inhabitants is not covered (abstractions for self-supply).

Slovak Republic. Freshwater resources: do not include underground flows (estimated at 946 million m^3). Irrigation data before 2000 include estimates.

Spain. Totals exclude abstractions for aquaculture.

Switzerland. Total renewable resources: exclude inflows from Liechtenstein (about 1%). Freshwater abstractions: partial totals excluding all agricultural uses. Data for 2012 include estimates.

Turkey. Totals are estimated on the basis of partial inventories, excluding agricultural uses other than irrigation and, until 1993, electrical cooling.

United Kingdom. Data refer to England and Wales only. Financial year (April to March) until 2000, and from 2008 onwards. Breaks in series in 1991 and 1999 (changes in reporting methods and classifications). Public supply: data include estimates.

OECD. Time series data include Secretariat estimates based on linear interpolations. OECD totals for water abstraction exclude Chile.

Population connected to wastewater treatment plants

"Connected" means actually connected to a wastewater treatment plant through a public sewage network. It does not take into account independent private facilities (e.g. septic tanks), used where public systems are not economic. The optimal connection rate is not necessarily 100%; it may vary among countries and depends on geographical features and on the spatial distribution of habitats.

- Primary treatment: physical and/or chemical process involving settlement of suspended solids, or other process in which the BOD5 of the incoming wastewater is reduced by at least 20% before discharge and the total suspended solids are reduced by at least 50%.
- Secondary treatment: process generally involving biological treatment with a secondary settlement or other process, with a BOD removal of at least 70% and a COD removal of at least 75%.
- Tertiary treatment: treatment of nitrogen and/or phosphorous and/or any other pollutant affecting the quality or a specific use of water (microbiological pollution, colour, etc.).

Chile. Data refer to population living in urban areas only. Include 2009 data for independent treatment.

Finland. Secondary treatment: 50-80% removal of BOD. Tertiary treatment: 70-90% removal of BOD.

France. Break in time series between 2004 and 2011.

Germany. Since 2007, total treatment includes population with storage tanks and transport to treatment plants by trucks, and "no treatment" refers to pre-treatment in independent treatment plants but with connection to the wastewater collecting system.

Greece. Data refer to agglomerations with more than 2000 population equivalent.

Ireland. Before 1999, data exclude some agglomerations of less than 2 000 population equivalents (p.e.). Since 1999, data refer to urban wastewater treatment delivered to agglomerations greater than or equal to 500 p.e. In 2011, data include agglomerations of less than 500 p.e. Before 2011, the population connected to on-site wastewater treatment installations (such as septic tanks) is not included.

Italy. Sewage connection rates are overestimated because it is assumed that the public sewerage serves the entire municipal population.

Japan. Secondary treatment may include some primary and tertiary treatment.

Korea. Population connected: includes population connected to public sewage treatment by pipe and some independent treatment.

Mexico. Estimates based on treated wastewater volumes.

Poland. Data also include population not connected by pipe, whose wastewater is collected in septic tanks and delivered to urban wastewater treatment plants by truck.

Portugal. Connection rates also cover preliminary treatment, undefined treatment and collective septic tanks.

Spain. Data refer to urban agglomerations of more than 2 000 population equivalent (p.e., approximately 1 300 inhabitants) and to estimates for agglomerations of less than 2 000 p.e. Systems of septic tanks are included in urban wastewater treatment. Connection rates may thus be overestimated.

Sweden. Break in series in 2000. Based on register studies on wastewater conditions in rural areas, it is assumed that everybody living in urban areas is connected to a wastewater treatment plant.

Turkey. Break in series in 2010. Before 2010, data referred only to municipalities; after 2010, also to villages.

United Kingdom. England and Wales only.

Threatened species

- "Threatened" refers to the sum of the "endangered", "critically endangered" and "vulnerable" species, i.e. species in danger of extinction and species soon likely to be in danger of extinction. Extinct species are excluded unless otherwise specified.
- "Endangered": species that are not "critically endangered" but face a very high risk of extinction in the wild in the near future.
- "Critically endangered": species that face an extremely high risk of extinction in the wild in the immediate future.
- "Vulnerable": species that are not "critically endangered" or "endangered" but face a high risk of extinction in the wild in the medium term.

It should be noted that the number of species known does not always accurately reflect the number of species in existence, and that countries apply the definitions with varying degrees of rigour.

For some countries, data include extinct species: the Czech Republic, and Greece (vascular plants).

Birds: for some countries the data refer to breeding species only (Austria, Belgium, Czech Republic, Denmark, France, Germany, Iceland, Luxembourg, the Netherlands, the Slovak Republic, Switzerland, United Kingdom).

Australia. Mammals: includes monotremes and marsupials.

Denmark. Vascular plants: apomictic species in the genus *hieracieum*, *rubus* and *taraxacum* are not included.

Finland. Vascular plants: include indigenous species and established aliens; exclude apomictic species and casual aliens.

France. Metropolitan France. Birds: species wintering, breeding and other regular visitors and passage migrants, indigenous species refer to breeding species only. Vascular plants: *angiospermae*, *gymnospermae* and *pteridophyta*.

Greece. Vascular plants: include 8 extinct species. Mammals: exclude marine mammals; the share threatened is underestimated.

Iceland. Mammals: terrestrial species only. Birds: about 350 species have been recorded one or more times on national territory.

Israel. Threatened indigenous mammals: data refer to 3 indigenous species that are all threatened.

Luxembourg. Vascular plants: species known are estimated based on the total number of taxons of the red list.

Mexico. Data are estimated. Indigenous: endemic species only. Birds: resident and migratory species. Vascular plants: pteridophytes, gymnosperms and angiosperms.

New Zealand. Threatened: national standard; indigenous species only. Known species exclude vagrants and migrant.

Norway. Species known: include only species that breed in Norway.

Portugal. Data include Azores and Madeira Islands. Birds: species assessed exclude vagrants.

Slovak Republic. Mammals: species known refer to taxons. Vascular plants: trees only.

Spain. Birds: indigenous birds include breeding species only. Vascular plants: the share of threatened species is estimated.

Sweden. Indigenous species only.

Switzerland. Assessed species.

United Kingdom. Indigenous species only. Threatened: national standard.

United States. Threatened: national definitions based on NatureServe Global Status Ranks. Species known: "indigenous" and "exotic" species.

Protected areas

Protected areas are areas of land and/or sea especially dedicated to the protection and maintenance of biological diversity and of natural and associated cultural resources, and managed through legal or other effective means. The data refer to IUCN management categories I-VI. National classifications may differ.

IUCN management categories I-VI:

Ia: strict nature reserves, managed mainly for science.

Ib: wilderness areas, managed mainly for wilderness protection.

II: national parks, managed mainly for ecosystem protection and recreation.

III: natural monuments, managed mainly for conservation of specific natural features.

IV: habitat/species management areas, managed mainly for habitat and species conservation through management intervention.

V: protected landscapes/seascapes, managed mainly for landscape/seascape conservation and recreation.

VI: managed resource protected areas, managed mainly for the sustainable use of natural ecosystems.

Australia. Includes the Great Barrier Reef Marine Park.

Denmark. Excludes Greenland.

France. Metropolitan France only.

Netherlands. Excludes the Netherlands Antilles.

Norway. Excludes Svalbard, Jan Mayen and Bouvet islands.

Portugal. Includes Azores and Madeira.

Spain. Includes Baleares and Canaries.

United Kingdom. Excludes overseas territories

United States. Includes Alaska. Excludes American Samoa, Guam, Minor Outlying Islands, Northern Mariana Islands, Puerto Rico and Virgin Islands.

Forest resources

Forest land

Forest land refers to land area spanning more than 0.5 ha and a canopy cover of more than 10%, or trees able to reach these thresholds *in situ*. It excludes woodland or forest predominantly under agricultural or urban land use and that used only for recreation.

Intensity of use of forest resources

- Intensity of use: refer to actual harvest or fellings divided by the annual productive capacity (gross increment).
- Fellings: average annual standing volume of all trees, living or dead, measured overbark to a minimum diameter of 0 cm (d.b.h.) that are felled during the given reference period, including the volume of trees or part of trees that are not removed from the forest, other wooded land or other felling site.
- Gross increment: average annual volume of increment over the reference period of all trees, measured to a minimum diameter breast height (d.b.h) of 0 cm.
- 2013: 2013 or latest available year (years prior to 2009 were not considered).

Austria. Annual averages over several years.

Denmark. Break in time series in 2012.

Estonia. Annual averages over several years. 1950-95: total forest including other wooded land and trees outside the forests. Since 2000: forest available for wood supply.

Finland. All forests are included.

France. Data refer to volumes removed from the forest, i.e. fellings plus dead wood harvested. Operating losses excluded.

Iceland. No data presented, as there is no traditional forestry in the country.

Netherlands. Before 2013, data refer to 5-year averages.

New Zealand. Gross increment: data from planted production forests only.

Portugal. Data are estimates.

Sweden. The area of forest available for wood supply has steadily decreased from 1990 as a result of environmental considerations including the establishment of formally and informally protected areas.

Forestry products as % of national exports of goods

- Ratio based on data expressed in monetary terms.
- Forestry products refer to wood forest products: roundwood, fuel wood and charcoal, industrial roundwood, sawn wood, wood-based panels, wood residue, and pulp for paper and paperboard.

Fish resources

- Total fish captures: fish production from capture fisheries; the data refer to nominal catches (landings converted to a live weight basis). Excluded are: aquatic plants, miscellaneous aquatic products, crocodiles, whales, seals and other aquatic mammals.
- Aquaculture refer to the farming of aquatic organisms with some sort of intervention in the rearing process to enhance production, such as regular stocking, feeding, protection from predators, etc.

Municipal waste

- Municipal waste refers to household and similar waste collected by or on behalf of municipalities. It includes waste originating from households and similar waste from small commercial activities, office buildings, institutions such as schools and government buildings, municipal services, and small businesses that dispose of waste at the same facilities used for municipally collected waste. It does not include municipal construction waste, nor waste sludges from municipal sewage treatment facilities.
- National definitions may differ. For some countries the data may include small amounts of special waste or waste electrical and electronic equipment (WEEE), or amounts of waste collected by the private sector, not on behalf of municipalities, in the framework of extended producer responsibility schemes. The inclusion of such amounts may lead to an overestimation of the amounts generated compared to the amounts reported by other countries.
- Disposal and recovery shares do not necessarily add up to 100%, because residue from some treatment operations (incineration, composting) are landfilled and because treatment operations other than those presented may not be covered.
- Recycling is defined as any reprocessing of material in a production process that diverts it from the waste stream, except reuse as fuel. Both reprocessing as the same type of product, and for different purposes are included. Direct recycling within industrial plants at the place of generation are excluded.
- Composting is defined as a biological process that submits biodegradable waste to anaerobic or aerobic decomposition, and that results in a product that is recovered.

Data refer to 2013 or the latest available year. The percentage changes are expressed with respect to 1990 and 2000, or to the closest available years. It should be noted that changes in definitions and methodologies create breaks in time series for several countries. When possible the periods used to calculate the percentage changes have been adapted to avoid these breaks in the calculation. See Tables A.2 and A.3 below for details about the years and periods covered.

Austria. Municipal waste: excludes construction site waste and green waste from municipal services that is composted on-site, which are included in the national definition. Waste from households: includes a small part of waste from commerce and trade.

Belgium. Waste from households: includes waste from small enterprises.

Canada. Percentage change: refers to household waste only. In 2010, 965 kg/capita of non-hazardous waste was generated from households, institutions, commercial establishments and industries (including construction and demolition waste). Disposal and recovery shares: estimates based on the above non-hazardous waste.

Chile. The share landfilled includes "other disposal".

Estonia. Data exclude packaging waste separately collected for recycling and thus under estimate the amount of municipal waste generated compared to other European countries.

France. Data include non-metropolitan areas (DOM, oversea departments). Recycling: before 2010, data refer to amount entering facilities; after 2010, they refer to amounts leaving facilities.

Germany. Share of incineration without energy recovery: include other disposal.

Greece. Landfill: as of 2010, includes amounts previously sent to uncontrolled dumping areas that were closed in 2009.

Hungary. Municipal waste generated: includes estimates for population not served by municipal waste services. Disposal and recovery: percentage based on collected amounts. Recycling: includes waste exported for recycling.

Ireland. Waste from households: includes estimates for households not served by waste collection. Disposal and recovery: include waste exported for treatment.

Italy. Composting: includes anaerobic treatments. Incineration with energy recovery: includes waste sent to industrial plants to produce energy (cement plants). Landfill: includes waste from sorting operations that is sent to landfill.

Japan. Municipal waste: data cover municipal collection, waste directly delivered and in-house treatment; exclude separate collection for recycling by private sector. Disposal and recovery shares: based on waste treated by municipalities and separate collection for recycling by private sector. Recycling: amounts directly recycled (including private collection) and recovered from intermediate processing.

Luxembourg. Recycling: around 97% of the non-organic municipal waste recycled is exported for treatment.

Mexico. Landfill: controlled, non-controlled and open landfills.

New Zealand. Data refer to amount going to landfill.

Norway. Per capita amounts based on population served by municipal waste services. Landfill: includes residues from other operations.

Poland. Waste generated: country estimates.

Portugal. Includes Azores and Madeira Islands. Recycling: separate collection.

Slovenia. Recycling: includes waste exported for recycling; excludes waste imported for recycling. Landfill: includes residues from other treatment operations.

Spain. Data include Baleares and Canary Islands. Recycling: separately collected amounts.

Sweden. Composting: includes on-site composting of kitchen, canteen, park and garden waste.

Turkey. Includes estimates for population not served by municipal waste services. Recycling and composting: refers to composting only.

United Kingdom. Waste from households: includes hazardous and clinical waste from households and waste from municipal services from street cleansing and litter bins.

OECD. Data are estimated: may differ from the sum of national data presented. Disposal and recovery: does not include Australia, Canada and Israel.

Table A.2. **Municipal waste generation**

Year or period shown

	Municipal waste generated per capita			*Of which:* From households
	Kg/cap	% change 1990-2013[a]	% change 2000-13[a]	Kg/cap
Australia	2009	1992-2009	2000-09	..
Austria	2012	1990-2012	2000-12	2012
Belgium	2013	1990-2013	2000-13	..
Canada	..	..	..	2010

Table A.2. **Municipal waste generation** *(cont.)*

Year or period shown

	Municipal waste generated per capita			*Of which:* From households
	Kg/cap	% change 1990-2013[a]	% change 2000-13[a]	Kg/cap
Chile	2009	1990-2009	2000-09	2009
Czech Republic	2013	..	2000-13	2013
Denmark	2013	..	2000-10	2013
Estonia	2013	..	..	..
Finland	2013	..	2000-13	2013
France	2013	1992-2013	2000-13	2013
Germany	2013	1990-2013	2000-13	2013
Greece	2012	1990-2009	2000-09	..
Hungary	2013	..	2000-13	2013
Iceland	2013	..	2000-13	..
Ireland	2012	..	2003-12	2012
Israel	2013	..	2000-13	..
Italy	2013	1991-2013	2000-13	..
Japan	2010	1990-2010	2000-10	2010
Korea	2012	1992-2012	2000-12	2012
Luxembourg	2013	..	2000-13	2013
Mexico	2012	1993-2012	2000-12	2012
Netherlands	2013	1990-2013	2000-13	2013
New Zealand	2013	1990-2011	2002-11	..
Norway	2013	..	2001-13	2013
Poland	2013	..	..	..
Portugal	2013	1990-2013	2000-13	..
Slovak Republic	2013	..	2002-13	2013
Slovenia	2013	..	..	2013
Spain	2013	..	2000-13	..
Sweden	2013	1990-2013	2000-13	..
Switzerland	2013	1990-2013	2000-13	2013
Turkey	2013	..	..	..
United Kingdom	2013	1990-2013	2000-13	2013
United States	2012	1990-2012	2000-12	2012
OECD	**2013**	**1990-2013**	**2000-13**	**..**
OECD America	2013	1990-2013	2000-13	..
OECD Asia-Oceania	2013	1990-2013	2000-13	..
OECD Europe	2013	1990-2013	2000-13	..

a) The periods used to calculate the percentage changes have been adapted to avoid that breaks in time series affect the calculation.

Table A.3. **Municipal waste disposal and recovery shares**

Year or period shown

	% of amounts treated	% change since 2000[a]	
		Recycling and composting	Landfill
Australia	2009	break	2003-09
Austria	2012	2000-12	2000-12
Belgium	2013	2000-13	2000-13
Canada	2010	2002-10	2002-10
Chile	2009	2000-09	2000-09
Czech Republic	2013	..	..
Denmark	2013	2000-10	2000-10
Estonia	2011	2000-11	2001-11
Finland	2013	2000-13	2000-13
France	2013	2000-13	2000-13
Germany	2013	2000-13	2000-13

Table A.3. **Municipal waste disposal and recovery shares** *(cont.)*

Year or period shown

	% of amounts treated	% change since 2000[a]	
		Recycling and composting	Landfill
Greece	2012	2000-12	2000-09
Hungary	2013	..	..
Iceland	2013	2000-13	2000-13
Ireland	2012	2000-12	2000-12
Israel	2013	2004-13	2004-13
Italy	2013	..	..
Japan	2010	2000-10	2000-10
Korea	2012	2000-12	2000-12
Luxembourg	2013	2000-13	2000-13
Mexico	2012	2000-12	2000-12
Netherlands	2013	..	..
New Zealand	2013	..	..
Norway	2013	2001-13	2001-13
Poland	2013	2000-10	2000-13
Portugal	2013	2000-13	2000-13
Slovak Republic	2013	..	..
Slovenia	2013	2000-13	2000-13
Spain	2013	..	..
Sweden	2013	2000-13	2000-13
Switzerland	2013	2000-13	2000-13
Turkey	2013	2000-13	2000-13
United Kingdom	2013	2000-13	2000-13
United States	2012	2000-12	2000-12
OECD	**2013**	**2000-13**	**2000-13**
OECD Europe	2013	2000-13	2000-13

a) The periods used to calculate the percentage changes have been adapted to avoid that breaks in time series affect the calculation.

Energy

Total primary energy supply (TPES)

TPES is made up of *production + imports – exports – international marine bunkers – international aviation bunkers ± stock changes*. Primary energy comprises coal, peat and peat products, oil shale, natural gas, crude oil and oil products, nuclear, and renewable energy (bioenergy, geothermal, hydropower, ocean, solar and wind). Electricity trade is also included in total primary energy supply, but excluded from the calculation of the breakdown by source.

GDP expressed in USD at 2005 prices and PPPs.

Australia. Excludes overseas territories.

Denmark. Excludes Greenland and the Danish Faroes.

France. Includes Monaco, and excludes the following overseas departments and territories: Guadeloupe, French Guiana, Martinique, New Caledonia, French Polynesia, Reunion, and St.-Pierre and Miquelon.

Italy. Includes San Marino and the Vatican.

Japan. Includes Okinawa.

Netherlands. Excludes Suriname, Aruba and the former Netherlands Antilles.

Portugal. Includes the Azores and Madeira.

Spain. Includes the Canary Islands.

Switzerland. Includes oil data for Liechtenstein.

United Kingdom. Shipments of coal and oil to the Channel Islands and the Isle of Man from the United Kingdom are not classed as exports. Supplies of coal and oil to these islands are, therefore, included as part of UK supply. Exports of natural gas to the Isle of Man are included with the exports to Ireland.

United States. Includes the 50 states and the District of Columbia. Oil statistics and coal trade statistics also include Puerto Rico, Guam, the Virgin Islands, American Samoa, Johnston Atoll, Midway Islands, Wake Island and the Northern Mariana Islands.

World. Data refer to 2013.

End-use prices

Prices are expressed in USD at current prices and exchange rates. Prices for natural gas are expressed per gross calorific value (GCV). The data refer to the year 2014, unless otherwise specified below.

Austria. 2013 data for natural gas (households).

Canada. 2013 data for natural gas and electricity (industry and households).

Chile. 2013 data.

Finland. 2011 data for natural gas (households).

Germany. 2013 data for natural gas (industry) and electricity (industry and households).

Greece. 2013 data for electricity (industry and households).

Israel. 2013 data for electricity (industry and households) and 2011 data for natural gas (households).

Italy. 2011 data for natural gas (households).

Japan. 2013 data for natural gas (industry and households).

Korea. 2013 data for natural gas (industry and households).

Luxembourg. 2013 data for natural gas and electricity (industry and households).

Netherlands. 2013 data for electricity (households).

New Zealand. 2013 data for natural gas (industry and households), 2012 and 2013 data for electricity (industry and households).

Norway. 2011 data for natural gas (households).

Spain. 2011 data for electricity (industry and households).

Sweden. 2013 data for light fuel oil (households).

United Kingdom. 2013 data for light fuel oil and electricity (industry).

Transport

Road traffic

Traffic volumes are expressed in billions of kilometres travelled by road vehicles; they are usually estimates and represent the average annual distance covered by vehicles, in kilometres, multiplied by the number of vehicles in operation. In principle, the data refer to the whole distance travelled on the whole network inside the national boundaries by national vehicles, with the exception of two- and three-wheeled vehicles, motorcycles, agricultural tractors, caravans and trailers.

The interpretation should take into account differences in the definition of road traffic volumes, such as the inclusion or exclusion of kilometres travelled on national territory by foreign vehicles, and variations in the method of estimation.

Data include Secretariat estimates and provisional data.

GDP data are expressed in USD at 2005 prices and PPPs.

Data refer to 2014 or to the latest available year. Data older than 2009 are not taken into consideration. The percentage changes are expressed with respect to 1990 and/or 2000, or to the closest available years (two years back and forth with respect to 1990 and 2000).

United Kingdom. Break in series in 1992.

United States. Data refer to passenger cars, motorcycles, light trucks, commercial freight vehicles and buses.

OECD. OECD totals are based on Secretariat estimates, and do not include Chile.

Motor vehicles

- Total stock of road motor vehicles: data include passenger cars, goods vehicles, buses and coaches; they refer to autonomous road vehicles with four or more wheels, excluding caravans and trailers, military vehicles, special vehicles (for emergency services, construction machinery, etc.) and agricultural tractors.
- Private car ownership is expressed as passenger cars per capita. Data refer to road motor vehicles, other than a motor cycle, intended for the carriage of passengers and designed to seat no more than nine persons (including the driver), including microcars (need no permit to be driven), taxis and hired passenger cars, provided that they have fewer than ten seats.
- Goods vehicles: data refer to vans, lorries (trucks) and road tractors. Excluded are caravans, trailers and semi-trailers, military or special vehicles, and agricultural tractors.

Australia. Goods vehicle: refers to light commercial vehicles, rigid trucks, articulated trucks and other trucks.

Canada. The total refers to all vehicles. Goods vehicles: refer to vans, trucks of 4.5 tonnes and over.

Belgium. Goods vehicles: include special vehicles, all-terrain vehicles and tankers.

Czech Republic. Goods vehicles: refer to lorries and road tractors.

Estonia. The total includes special vehicles. Goods vehicles refer to lorries and special vehicles.

Germany. Passenger cars: break in series in 2007.

Hungary. Passenger cars: break in series in 1996.

Iceland. Goods vehicles: refers to lorries and vans.

Israel. The total includes special vehicles.

Luxembourg. Passenger cars: include mixed-use vehicles.

New Zealand. Passenger cars: include vans.

Poland. The total is the sum of passenger cars, lorries and buses.

United States. Light trucks include vans, pickup trucks and sport utility vehicles. The total is the sum of light duty vehicles, short wheel base, motorcycle, light duty vehicle, long wheel base, truck, single-unit 2-axle 6-tire or more, trucks and buses.

OECD. Totals are based on Secretariat estimates.

Road network

- Total road network: includes all roads in a given area. "Roads" refers to motorways, main or national highways, secondary or regional roads, and others. In principle, the data refer to all public roads, streets and paths in urban and rural areas, excluding private roads, and describe the situation on 31 December of each year.

- Motorways: class of roads, specifically designed and built for motor traffic, which does not serve properties bordering on it, and which: a) is provided, except at special points or temporarily, with separate carriageways for the two directions of traffic, separated from each other, either by a dividing strip not intended for traffic, or exceptionally by other means; b) does not cross at level with any road, railway or tramway track, or footpath; and c) is especially sign-posted as a motorway and is reserved for specific categories of road motor vehicles.

Australia. Motorways: the methodology has changed with respect to previously published data (no time series available).

Canada. Total road network: two-lane equivalent thousand km.

Iceland. Total road network: includes national, major, collector (distributor), country and highland roads.

Mexico. Motorways: refers to roads with 4 or more lanes.

Netherlands. Motorways: break in series in 2001.

Spain. Total road network: excludes "other" roads.

Switzerland. Total road network: includes cantonal and municipal roads and national highways except motorways.

United States. Total road network: refers to all roads (paved and unpaved). Motorways: refers to roads with 4 or more lanes.

OECD. Totals are based on Secretariat estimates.

Road fuel prices and taxes

- Taxes: includes taxes that have to be paid by the consumer as part of the transaction and are not refundable.
- Diesel fuel: diesel for commercial use.
- Unleaded gasoline: unleaded premium (95 RON) except as noted.
- Prices: expressed in USD at 2005 prices and PPP.

Chile. Gasoline: 2013 data.

Japan. Gasoline: regular unleaded.

Agriculture

Commercial fertilisers

The intensity of use of fertilisers is expressed as the apparent consumption of fertilisers for agriculture production (in nutrient contents). The apparent consumption *equals* production *plus* imports *minus* non-fertiliser use *minus* exports. Apparent consumption figures are developed based on the underlying assumption that supply equals consumption.

The data are sourced from FAO. They build on official country data. In the case where official data were not available from the country for certain products or certain years, reliable information from other sources was used for the period not covered by official data. Detailed country data was analysed for building a harmonised trend in the time series on total production, imports, exports, and consumption, starting with the year 2002.

All figures are calculated in weight of plant nutrients. Nitrogen is generally expressed in the elemental form (N). Phosphate is expressed as the oxide form P_2O_5.

Livestock density

Livestock densities are estimated and expressed as the number of live animals (in sheep equivalent heads) per hectare of agricultural land. The data include sheep, goats, pigs, asses, mules, horses, cattle, buffaloes and poultry birds. The coefficients used to convert to sheep equivalents are: cattle = 6; sheep and Goats = 1; horses = 4.8; pigs = 1, poultry birds = 0.06. *Source:* FAO.

Organic farming

Agricultural land includes arable land, permanent crops and permanent meadows and pastures.

The agricultural land under organic farming includes areas under certified organic farming and areas in conversion to organic farming. Areas under certified organic farming refer to the area of "arable land" exclusively dedicated to organic agriculture and managed by applying organic agriculture methods. It is the portion of land area managed (cultivated) or wild harvested in accordance with specific organic standards or technical regulations and that has been inspected and approved by a certification body. *Source:* FAO.

Israel. Data refer to certified organic farming.

Agricultural production

The agricultural production index is based on the sum of price-weighted quantities of different agricultural commodities produced, after deductions of quantities used as seed and feed weighted in a similar manner. The resulting aggregate represents, therefore, disposable production for any use, except as seed and feed. All the indices shown at the country, regional and world levels are calculated by the Laspeyres formula. They may differ from those produced by the countries themselves because of differences in concepts of production, coverage, weights, time reference of data and methods of calculation. *Source:* FAO (see FAOSTAT for more details).

Environmentally related taxation

Environmentally related tax revenue is expressed as a percentage of total tax revenue and percentage of GDP. Environmentally related taxes include taxes on:

- Energy products for transport purposes (gasoline and diesel) and for stationary purposes (fossil fuels and electricity).
- Motor vehicles and transport, i.e. one-off import or sales taxes, recurrent taxes on registration or road use and other transport taxes.
- Other environmentally related taxes include taxes on waste management (final disposal, packaging and other waste-related product taxes), ozone-depleting substances and other environmentally related taxes that could not be allocated among these fields.

Data refer to the year 2013 or the latest available year; data prior to 2010 were not considered. Changes are calculated from the year 2000 or from the first available year (after 2000); data posterior to 2003 were not considered for the calculation of the change.

Environmentally related tax revenue as % total tax revenue: for some countries, the latest available year for this indicator is 2012, due to missing data on total tax revenue (Australia, Japan, Mexico, Netherlands, Poland).

Monetary values are expressed in million USD at 2005 prices and PPPs.

OECD. Data refer to the weighted average of all OECD countries.

Environmentally related R&D

Public environmentally related R&D

The data refer to Government Budget Appropriations or Outlays for Research and Development (GBAORD), that measure the funds that governments allocate to R&D to meet various socio-economic objectives. These objectives are based on the Nomenclature for the Analysis and Comparison of Scientific Programmes and Budgets (NABS 2007). The indicator presented refers to the socio-economic objective "environment", which includes research directed at the control of pollution and at developing monitoring facilities to measure, eliminate and prevent pollution. It is expressed as a percentage of all-purpose GBAORD. Details can be found in OECD (2015), *Frascati Manual 2015: Guidelines for Collecting and Reporting Data on Research and Experimental Development*, "The Measurement of Scientific and Technological Activities", OECD Publishing, Paris, *http://dx.doi.org/10.1787/9789264239012-en*.

Estimates of environmentally-related government R&D are reported from the primary funder perspective, i.e. as budgets rather than as expenditure from the performer perspective. Estimated budgets and actual expenditures by governments might differ because projected amounts of R&D at the appropriations stage vary from what is actually measured by the performers of the R&D. Differences may also be due to an imprecision in the budget appropriations that impede the identification of appropriations that are specifically targeted at R&D.

Monetary values are expressed in million USD at 2005 prices and PPPs.

Data refer to two-year averages (2012-13) or the latest available average, data prior to 2010 were not considered. Changes are calculated from the 2000-01 average or from the first available average (after 2000), data posterior to 2003 were not considered for the calculation of the change.

For the **Czech Republic, Estonia** and **Poland,** the change is calculated from the 2001-02 average. For **Korea** and **Mexico,** the latest available average refers to 2011-12.

OECD. Data refer to the weighted average of the two-period country averages shown. The OECD average does not include Turkey, and the change from 2000-01 does not inlude Chile and Hungary.

Renewable energy RD&D

The data refer to public budgets directed at research, development and demonstration (RD&D) related to hydro, geothermal, solar (thermal and photovoltaic), wind and tide/wave/ocean energy, as well as combustible renewables (solid biomass, liquid biomass, biogas) and other renewable energy technologies (all supporting measuring, monitoring and verifying technologies in renewable energies). It is expressed as a percentage of total energy RD&D public budgets (directed at all forms of energy).

Total energy RD&D budgets of public entities (government, public agencies and state-owned enterprises, as defined by the IEA) cover research, (basic research oriented towards the development of energy-related technologies, and applied research), and development and demonstration related to the production, storage, transportation, distribution and rational use of all forms of energy. Deployment is excluded. They concern one of the following seven main branches of energy-related developments: i) energy efficiency; ii) fossil fuels (oil, gas and coal); iii) renewables; iv) nuclear fission and fusion; v) hydrogen and fuel cells; vi) other power and storage techniques; and vii) other cross-cutting technologies or research.

The data are sourced from International Energy Agency (IEA). As for GBAORD, estimates are reported from the funder perspective as budgets (rather than as expenditure from the performer perspective). The data on energy RD&D should however not be confused with the data on GBAORD allocated to the socio-economic objective "Production, distribution and rational utilisation of energy", which is a narrower concept defined in the Frascati Manual.

Data refer to two-year averages (2012-13) or the latest available average, data prior to 2010 were not considered. Changes are calculated from the 2000-01 average or from the first available average (after 2000), data posterior to 2003 were not considered for the calculation of the change.

Monetary values are expressed in million USD at 2005 prices and PPPs.

Czech Republic. Latest available data refers to the 2010-11 average, the change is calculated from the 2002-03 average.

For **Estonia, Greece, Italy, Japan** and **Korea,** the latest available average refers to 2011-12. For Ireland and Korea, the change is calculated from the 2001-02 average

OECD. Data refer to the weighted average of the two-period country averages shown. The OECD average does not include Chile, Iceland, Israel, Mexico and Slovenia. The change from 2000-01 excludes Estonia, Luxembourg, Poland and the Slovak Republic.

Environmentally related Official Development Assistance (ODA)

The OECD Development Assistance Committee (DAC) has established a comprehensive system for measuring aid targeting the environment, renewable energy and the objectives of the Rio Conventions. The DAC currently has 29 members, including 28 OECD member countries and the European Union.

ODA allocated to environmentally related sectors

The data refer to bilateral ODA and do not include core contributions by donors to multilateral organisations. They represent ODA allocated to environmentally related sectors expressed as a share of total sector-allocable ODA:

- The environment sector refers to general environmental protection activities, i.e. environmental policy and administrative management, biosphere protection, biodiversity, site preservation, flood prevention/control, environmental education/ training and environmental research.
- The water supply and sanitation sector refers to water sector policy and administrative management, water resources conservation, water supply and sanitation, basic drinking water supply and basic sanitation, river basin' development, waste management/ disposal, education and training in water supply and sanitation.
- The renewable energy sector refers to activities that promote the development and deployment of energy generation facilities with reduced pressure on the environment. It includes hydro-electric power plants, geothermal energy, solar energy, wind power, ocean power and biomass.

Sector-allocable ODA comprises aid directed to social infrastructure and services, economic infrastructure and services, production sectors and multi-sector/cross cutting aid. The data represent gross disbursements (not commitments), which best reflect efforts by donors. The sector of destination of the ODA does not refer to the type of goods or services provided by the donor, but to the sector of the recipient's economic structure that the transfer is intended to foster. Sector specific environmental activities are reported under the sector to which they are directed, not under the environmentally related sectors described above. For example, water related ODA such as dams and reservoirs for irrigation and hydropower, and activities related to river transport, are classed under *aid to agriculture*, *energy* and *transport*, respectively.

Data refer to the year 2013 or the latest available year, data prior to 2010 were not considered. Changes are calculated from 2002 or from 2003, data posterior to 2003 were not considered for the calculation of the change.

Denmark. The change for the 3 environmentally related sectors is calculated from the year 2003.

Greece. Data on renewable energy ODA refer to 2010.

Iceland. Data on the environment sector refer to 2012.

Italy. The change for renewable energy ODA is calculated from the year 2003.

Switzerland. The change for environment sector is calculated from the year 2003.

OECD. For each sector, data refers to the unweighted average of the information shown for all OECD member countries. This average includes non-DAC members (e.g. Estonia).

Net ODA

Net ODA is expressed as a percentage of Gross National Income (GNI). Net ODA consists of disbursements of loans made on concessional terms (net of repayments of principal) and grants to developing countries and territories on the OECD/DAC list of aid recipients that are undertaken by the official sector with promotion of economic development and welfare as the main objective. Technical co-operation is included. Grants, loans and credits for military purposes are excluded. Concessional loans are defined as loans with a grant element of at least 25 per cent (calculated at a rate of discount of 10 per cent).

Gross national income (GNI) is expressed at market prices and is the sum of gross primary incomes receivable by resident institutional units and sectors. In contrast to gross domestic product (GDP), GNI is a concept of income (primary income) rather than value added. GNI is equal to GDP (which at market prices represents the final result of the production activity of resident producer units) less taxes (less subsidies) on production and imports, compensation of employees and property income payable to the rest of the world plus the corresponding items receivable from the rest of the world.

The best known target in international aid, agreed in 1970, proposes to raise ODA to 0.7% of donors' national income. In 2005, the 15 countries that were members of the European Union by 2004 agreed to reach the target by 2015.

Net ODA as % of Gross National Income (GNI)

Data refer to the year 2013 or the latest available year, data prior to 2010 were not considered. Changes are calculated from the year 2000 or from the first available year (after 2000); data posterior to 2003 were not considered for the calculation of the change.

Hungary. Change is calculated from the year 2003.

OECD. Data refer to the unweighted average of the information shown for all OECD member countries. This average includes non-DAC members. The change is calculated excluding Slovenia.

ORGANISATION FOR ECONOMIC CO-OPERATION AND DEVELOPMENT

The OECD is a unique forum where governments work together to address the economic, social and environmental challenges of globalisation. The OECD is also at the forefront of efforts to understand and to help governments respond to new developments and concerns, such as corporate governance, the information economy and the challenges of an ageing population. The Organisation provides a setting where governments can compare policy experiences, seek answers to common problems, identify good practice and work to co-ordinate domestic and international policies.

The OECD member countries are: Australia, Austria, Belgium, Canada, Chile, the Czech Republic, Denmark, Estonia, Finland, France, Germany, Greece, Hungary, Iceland, Ireland, Israel, Italy, Japan, Korea, Luxembourg, Mexico, the Netherlands, New Zealand, Norway, Poland, Portugal, the Slovak Republic, Slovenia, Spain, Sweden, Switzerland, Turkey, the United Kingdom and the United States. The European Union takes part in the work of the OECD.

OECD Publishing disseminates widely the results of the Organisation's statistics gathering and research on economic, social and environmental issues, as well as the conventions, guidelines and standards agreed by its members.

OECD PUBLISHING, 2, rue André-Pascal, 75775 PARIS CEDEX 16
(97 2015 09 1 P) ISBN 978-92-64-23518-2 – 2015-01

www.ingramcontent.com/pod-product-compliance
Lightning Source LLC
LaVergne TN
LVHW080929120826
845149LV00018B/1772
* 9 7 8 9 2 6 4 2 3 5 1 8 2 *